Daily Telegraph

POCKET SPORTS FACTS

GOLF

MICHAEL WILLIAMS

T

Consultant Editor: Norman Barrett

Editor: Gill Freeman

Design: Nigel Standerline

Acknowledgements: The author and publishers wish to record their thanks for the help given by:
The Golfers' Handbook; The Guiness Book of Golf Facts and Feats (Donald Steel); Royal and Ancient Championship Records (Peter Ryde); PGA European Tour; Augusta National (Hazel Salmon); US Golf Association (Patrick Leany).

Designed and produced by
Autumn Publishing Ltd.,
10 Eastgate Square, Chichester,
West Sussex.

Published by Telegraph Publications,
135, Fleet Street,
London EC4P 4BL

Typesetting by Project Reprographics, Chichester.
Printed by CGP Delo, Yugoslavia.

ISBN 0 86367 016 4

Cover picture: Severiano Ballesteros

Picture credits:
Colorsport, BBC Hulton Picture Library

CONTENTS

INTRODUCTION

Golf is that rare, if not unique, game in which the player is the complete master of his own destiny. He has his own ball and his own clubs. The play of his opponent or opponents has no direct bearing on his own game. He can hit his shots in his own time with no interference. If his opponent has a birdie there is nothing to stop him, other than his own ability or lack of it, getting one as well.

Yet hitting a motionless ball from one point to another with any one of 14 clubs — the choice again is entirely up to the player — has driven countless thousands to despair for the percentage of those who have gained a degree of mastery at golf is minute.

Golf is rare, too, in that there are still two distinct categories of player, the amateur and the professional. For the professional, golf is now big business. There are now three one-million-dollar tournaments. In a career spanning 21 years Jack Nicklaus has won in official prize money well in excess of £3 million, which has almost certainly been doubled if not trebled by 'off course' earnings, which are negotiated by a player's manager. Sports management is now very much a part of professional golf.

Yet despite the huge sums of money involved, the game is still played in the same spirit as in days long since passed. It is doubtful whether there is a player in the world who would not willingly forfeit his prize money in return for winning the Open Championship. The honour, the prestige and the title still come first, which is as it should be.

This book therefore devotes itself more to what is called the major championships — the Open, US Open, Masters and American PGA than it does to tournament golf. These are the pinnacles of the game and a man is measured by his successes in them. It is the only true yardstick.

A selection of the great players was nevertheless not an easy one for they go back more than 100 years, their reputations and exploits having been passed on from generation to generation. A selection of the great courses was even harder. Unlike the players, they still exist, like Prestwick, where the first Open Championship of all was played in 1860.

One can therefore still sample the same stage where all the greats have played and put yourself in their shoes. There is no greater thrill than to stand on the first tee at St Andrews and it is remarkable how most of these courses have stood the passage of time, for all the improvements in the manufacture of equipment.

If I have omitted some outstanding courses, it is because I have neither seen them or played them. Royal County Down in Northern Ireland is an example. My choice was subjective rather than one by reputation alone.

The chapter on the rules is, I hope, a simplification to those whose interest in the game is purely one of enjoyment rather than competitive while the section on golfing terms exposes the extensive vocabulary of the game.

Above all this is a book that can be easily carried in the pocket and produced to verify a fact or two. It may even settle a wager or an argument.

Tom Watson (United States) — the joy of a winning putt.

THE BIG FOUR

When, in 1930, Bobby Jones won the British Amateur Championship, the British Open Championship, the American Open Championship and the American Amateur Championship (in that order), this cluster of unprecedented triumphs in the same year was immediately called the Grand Slam of golf.

Jones was, at the time, an amateur but the standards of professional play have improved so much since then that it is safe to say that such a feat is most unlikely ever to be repeated.

The Grand Slam remains to be conquered though the peaks of such an achievement have, of necessity, changed. Now it bridges the British and American Open Championships, the Masters and the American PGA. No man has yet won them all in the same year, though in 1953 Ben Hogan triumphed in the two Opens and in the Masters. A clash of dates prevented him from entering the PGA.

Four golfers have won these four 'majors', as they have become known, at least once, though in different years. They are Jack Nicklaus, whose collection of five Masters, five PGAs, four US Opens and three British Opens (in addition to two US Amateurs) is unrivalled, Ben Hogan, Gary Player and Gene Sarazen.

Jack Nicklaus (United States), with the Open trophy in 1978, one of his 17 'majors'.

THE OPEN CHAMPIONSHIP

This is the oldest championship of all, its origins going back to Prestwick in 1860, when eight professionals played three times round the then 12-hole course. Now the Open Championship (strictly speaking never the 'British Open') stands supreme, attracting a world-wide entry each year. The live television coverage has an audience running into many millions in all quarters of the globe.

Even the Americans, who naturally attach particular importance to their own US Open, do not regard themselves as complete golfers until they have won the Open. Originally this was because the links courses beside the sea, on which the championship is always played, presented an entirely different sort of test.

On unwatered fairways, with greens often burned brown by the sun, invariably in a wind, manipulation and control of the ball demanded skills entirely different from those required on the lush, man-made inland courses of America. In recent years the introduction of pop-up sprinklers round the greens and fairway watering may have reduced the number of unpredictable bounces but there are many who would still like to see a return to 'the old days'.

Organisation of the Open Championship was taken over by the Royal and Ancient, the game's governing body, in 1920. It was about this time that the Americans began making the trip to give the event true international status. Walter Hagen was the first American winner, at Royal St Georges, Sandwich, in 1922 and two more of that country's celebrated sons, Bobby Jones, the amateur, and Gene Sarazen, soon followed in his footsteps.

The famous old silver claret jug was frequently taken back across the Atlantic, whether by Hagen, who won four times, Jones, who won three, or by Britons who had gone to live in the States, like Jock Hutchison and Tommy Armour. It was not until 1934 that the invaders were finally repelled, Henry Cotton winning in style at Royal St George's. His second round of 65 stood for more than 40 years as the championship's lowest score, giving the name to the Dunlop 65 ball.

Cotton won twice more, in 1937 at Carnoustie and again at Muirfield in 1948. American interest had dwindled and was not revived by Sam Snead's victory at St Andrews in 1946, nor even immediately by Ben Hogan's meticulous dissection of Carnoustie in 1953, the year in which he had already won the US Open and Masters.

These were the years of Bobby Locke, a South African as well known for his plus fours as for the 'draw' with which he hit almost every shot, and Peter Thomson, a neat Australian of almost monotonous consistency. Locke won four times between 1949 and 1957 and Thomson five times between 1954 and 1965, including a hat-trick.

Thomson's fifth win at Royal Birkdale equalled the performances of JH Taylor between 1894 and 1913 and James Braid between 1901 and 1910. This has since been equalled by Tom Watson between 1975 and 1983. Harry Vardon's six victories between 1896 and 1914 still stand as the record, though only young Tom Morris, who gained his first victory in 1868, has triumphed four times in a row.

Hogan's victory, nevertheless, lit a long fuse and when the Centenary Open came along at St Andrews in 1960, Arnold Palmer, who was then at the height of his powers and winner that year of both the Masters and the US Open, decided he would challenge. He lost by a stroke to Kel Nagle, of Australia.

But Palmer was hooked. A year later he was back at Royal Birkdale and this time he won. Twelve months later he triumphed again, this time at Troon. Vast crowds, some paying customers and some not, swarmed all over the course and the Open Championship as we know it today was well and truly launched.

Since then the Americans have been crossing the Atlantic in full force as prize money, £7,000 in 1960, has increased to more than £300,000 in 1983. They have not had it all their own way, but mostly. Gary Player, of South Africa, triumphed in three different decades, 1959, 1968 and 1974, Roberto de Vicenzo, of Argentina, was a most popular winner at Hoylake in 1967, Tony Jacklin ended many barren British years with a fine victory at Lytham in 1969 (within 12 months he was also American champion) and in 1979 Severiano Ballesteros, of Spain, became the first continental champion since Arnaud Massy, of France, in 1907.

Its most dominating personality—despite Watson's five victories in nine years—has been Jack Nicklaus. Winner three times, in 1966, 1970 and 1978, he has also been runner-up or joint runner-up on seven occasions and altogether finished in the top five 16 times. Such distinction is without parallel.

UNITED STATES OPEN

Such is the size of the entry these days—somewhere between 4,000 and 5,000 each year—that the United States Open Championship has become less and less of an international event. The overseas entry is now very small for the chances of surviving the many qualifying rounds are as slight as they would be lengthy and therefore uneconomical for the hopeful visitor.

Since 1920 only three non-Americans have won the US

Open, Gary Player, of South Africa, in 1965, Tony Jacklin, of England, in 1970 and David Graham, of Australia, in 1981. This was not the case in the early years, at the turn of the century, when it was dominated by British professionals who had gone to live in the States.

First played at Newport, Rhode Island, in 1895, it was not until 1900 that the title first went abroad, Harry Vardon beating JH Taylor by two strokes at Chicago. By 1905 Willie Anderson had set a record that stands to this day—three successive victories—and in 1911 Johnny McDermott became America's first home-bred champion.

But the significant turning of the tide came two years later when a 20-year-old amateur, Francis Ouimet, beat the might of British professional golf, Vardon and Ted Ray, in a play-off at The Country Club, Brookline. Though Ray had his hour of glory at Inverness in 1920, the year 1913 has gone into the history books as the moment when Ouimet lit the American torch.

Apart from the isolated victories by Player, Jacklin and Graham, American domination has been complete. Bobby Jones (1923-26-29-30), Ben Hogan (1948-50-51-53) and Jack Nicklaus (1962-67-72-80) have all won four times, as did Anderson in 1901-03-04-05. Jones also has the distinction of being runner-up four times, as were Arnold Palmer and Sam Snead. Tantalisingly, it was a championship that eluded Snead throughout his career—the only gap in an otherwise distinguished career.

The Americans put their Open Championship before all else. It has certainly become the most difficult to win, not least because the United States Golf Association, who run the event, make their courses very demanding for the occasion, with punishing rough and very fast greens.

From time to time the suggestion has been made that the USGA should limit their rota of championship courses. But it is always rejected on the grounds that this is a national open and must serve the whole of America. So far 47 courses have played host.

The latest newcomer was Atlanta Athletic Club in 1976, this being the home town of Bobby Jones, who dominated the championship in the 1920s. His victory at Interlachen in 1930 provided the third leg of his historic Grand Slam of the British and American Open Championships and the British and American Amateur Championships.

Twelve months later came the longest US Open of all, Billy Burke and George von Elm tieing after 72 holes, tieing again after another 36 and Burke winning by a stroke after another 36 holes. Unlike the Masters and PGA, the championship has still, in the event of a tie, to be decided over 18 holes.

Snead lost his best chance of winning in 1939 when he took eight at the final hole at Philadelphia, though he did not know at the time that a five would have been sufficient. Soon after the war his great contemporary and rival, Ben Hogan, won his first US Open at Riviera.

But Hogan's greatest triumph was at Merion in 1950, not much more than a year after he had nearly lost his life in a car accident. On legs still giving him considerable pain, he won in a play-off against Lloyd Mangrum and George Fazio.

Hogan won twice more, successfully defending the title at Oakland Hills where he vowed he would bring 'this monster to its knees,' and at Oakmont in 1953. He was also beaten in a play-off two years later by Jack Fleck, a club professional from Iowa.

But a new hero was emerging, Arnold Palmer producing one of his famous 'charges', came from seven strokes behind in the last round to win at Cherry Hills in 1960. It was his only championship victory. Two years later Jack Nicklaus, still in his first year as a professional, beat him in a play-off at Oakmont, as did Billy Casper at Olympic in 1966. At one point in the final round Palmer had led Casper by seven strokes.

When Jack Nicklaus won at Baltusrol in 1980, setting incidentally, a record aggregate of 272, the interval between his first and now his fourth victory spanned 18 years, another record. His opening round of 63, together with that by Tom Weiskopf, equalled the lowest in a US Open, the other being by Johnny Miller at Oakmont in 1973. But Miller's was in the fourth round and therefore won him the most spectacular victory of all time.

THE MASTERS

The Masters is the only one of the four major championships that is always played on the same course, Augusta National, in Georgia. The man behind the birth of the tournament, and the course, was Bobby Jones. He always insisted it was called a 'tournament' even though it has come to be classified as a championship.

His influence on the event—together with that of his close friend Clifford Roberts—remains to this day. No advertising is allowed on the course and there is not even a programme, only a single sheet of paper with the starting times on one side and a map of the course on the other.

This is an echo of the earliest days of the Masters, the first, in 1934, being no more than a gathering of a few old friends of Jones'. Indeed to create some local interest, Jones himself came out of retirement, though the first champion was Horton Smith.

He was promptly made an honorary member of a club with one of the smallest and most exclusive memberships in

America. This practice has been continued and at the prize-giving each year the new champion is presented by the immediate past champion with a green jacket, or blazer, bearing the distinctive crest of Augusta National.

In recent years the past champions have been given their own private locker room. They also receive a life-long invitation to play in the tournament, or at least to attend, though the field is still restricted to between 70 and 80 each year. Now invitation is by qualification, among Americans. In addition, a few selected overseas players are included, such as the British Amateur champion.

While the first Masters may have needed publicity, the second got it of its own accord when Gene Sarazen, three strokes behind Craig Wood with four holes to play, had an albatross two at the 15th, a par five. Sarazen tied and then won the play-off over 18 holes.

Such was the publicity attached to this single shot that the tournament never looked back. Admission is now by advance ticket sales only, while such is the television coverage that even those who have never been to Augusta are familiar with the spectacularly scenic holes on land that was once a nursery.

It was soon after the second world war that the Masters gained the status of a major championship, Sam Snead winning in 1949, 1952 and 1954 and Ben Hogan in 1951 and 1953. In 1954 Hogan tied with Snead but lost the play-off. They were then the two best golfers in the world.

But by 1958 Arnold Palmer was on the march. Two years later he won the title for a second time and in now typical fashion. He had birdie threes at both the 17th and 18th holes in the final round to beat Ken Venturi by a stroke.

Palmer's third victory was in 1962, but only after a play-off. He had tied with Gary Player who, 12 months earlier, had become the first overseas player to win the Masters. In the additional 18 holes necessary to find a champion, Palmer played the inward half in 31 for a 68 to beat both Player and Dow Finsterwald.

After another two years Palmer won yet again but in the meantime (1963) Jack Nicklaus had already begun his 'take over'. At 23, he was the youngest champion—until Severiano Ballesteros, who was only a matter of two months younger when he triumphed for the first time in 1980.

Nicklaus passed Palmer's tally of four victories by winning in 1963-65-66-72-75. That in 1965, when he had a 72-hole total of 271 (later equalled by Raymond Floyd in 1976) drew from Bobby Jones the comment: 'Mr Nicklaus plays a game with which I am not familiar'.

His winning margin of nine strokes that year still stands as the record. But the lowest last round to win the championship was recorded by Player in 1978—a 64. This was his second Masters. Ballesteros has since joined him (in

1980 and 1983) as only the second overseas champion—and the first of course from Europe.

In more recent years, play-offs have been reduced to sudden death beginning at the 10th hole. The first winner in a sudden-death finish was Fuzzy Zoeller in 1979. He is the only player to have become champion in his first Masters appearance while the best remembered loser was Roberto de Vicenzo in 1968. In the final round he signed for a four instead of the birdie three he had scored at the 17th. He consequently lost by a stroke to Bob Goalby.

THE PGA

Without in any way wishing to be disrespectful, the American PGA championship is the least celebrated of the four major championships. It is nevertheless the oldest event on the United States professional tour, having been founded in 1916.

Until 1957 the format was always match-play. In 1958 it reverted to 72 holes of stroke-play, the professional belief being that this is the fairest way of finding a champion. In match-play it is possible for someone to go round in 67 or less and lose while someone else can hole the course in 72 or more and still win. Such elements of chance are not popular.

Two players, Walter Hagen and Jack Nicklaus, have each won the PGA five times. Hagen's successes spanned seven years—between 1921 and 1927 and were all therefore in match-play—while Nicklaus won his first title in 1963 and, to date, his last in 1980, all by a stroke-play.

Nicklaus has also been runner-up four times, in 1964-65-74-83, more than anyone else. Byron Nelson, Billy Casper and Arnold Palmer each finished second three times, this being the only major championship to elude Palmer.

Now that the Tournament Players' Championship is being held each year at the Tournament Players' Club at Sawgrass, Florida, there is a possibility that this event could supplant the PGA in importance. However the TPC is played only a week or two before the Masters whereas the PGA is now held in August, a suitable interval after the British Open.

The first winner of the PGA was an Englishman, Jim Barnes, who was later to triumph in both the American and British Open Championships. He defeated a Scotsman, Jock Hutchinson, in the final at Siwanoy, New York and, at the conclusion of the first world war three years later, successfully defended his title.

Hagen became the first American-born winner of the title in 1921. He reached the final on the six successive occasions he competed. He did not defend in 1922, lost to Gene Sarazen (who had won in his absence) in 1923, and then won the championship four years in a row.

This was a remarkable period of domination by a player who was at his most formidable in the cut and thrust of match-play. When Hagen lost to Leo Diegel in the third round in 1928, it was his first defeat in 22 matches.

In 1932 Hagen was also involved in the longest match, losing to Johnny Golden at the 43rd hole at Keller, Minnesota. That same year also saw the bravest recovery. Bobby Cruickshank had been nine down with 12 to play against Al Watrous. Out of pity perhaps, Watrous had just given his opponent a six foot putt for a half, an act of generosity he was to regret as Cruickshank came back to win, though Ollin Dutra took the championship.

Sam Snead made five appearances in the final between 1938 and 1951. He lost the first two but won the last three. Byron Nelson also appeared in the final five times, between 1939 and 1945 but was defeated on three occasions.

Lionel Hebert was the last match-play champion in 1957 at Miami Valley, Ohio, and Dow Finsterwald, who had lost in the final, the first at stroke-play at Llanerch, Pennsylvania, the following year. In 1962 Jack Nicklaus finished third at his first attempt (three strokes behind Gary Player, who was winning the first of his two championships) but he triumphed 12 months later at Dallas Athletic Country Club.

A professional for less than two years, Nicklaus had already won two other majors, the US Open of 1962 and the Masters in the spring of 1963. He was still only 23 (not as young as Sarazen who was 20 when he won in 1922) but in 1968 Julius Boros became the oldest champion. He was 48 when he finished a stroke ahead of Bob Charles at Pecan Valley, Texas.

In 1973 Nicklaus won for the third time. It was his 14th major championship and took him past Bobby Jones' total of 13. A fourth PGA title went on to his sideboard in 1975 while 1977 was notable for the first sudden-death play-off in a major championship. Lanny Wadkins defeated Gene Littler at the third extra hole at Pebble Beach.

There were play-offs in 1978 and 1979 as well, while in 1980 Nicklaus not only equalled Hagen's five victories but his seven-stroke margin from Andy Bean was a record.

WINNERS OF THE MAJOR EVENTS

THE FOUR MAJOR CHAMPIONSHIPS

Changes in the overall prize money for the tournament and the amount received by the winner, have been indicated on the results. Unfortunately, complete figures for the United States PGA are not available.

OPEN CHAMPIONSHIP

Players from Great Britain, unless otherwise stated. *amateur

1860 Prestwick
174 Willie Park 55-59-60
176 Tom Morris Snr 58-59-59
180 Andrew Strath
1861 Prestwick
163 Tom Morris Snr 54-56-53
167 Willie Park 54-54-59
171 William Dow 59-58-54
1862 Prestwick
163 Tom Morris 52-55-56
176 Willie Park 59-59-58
178 Charles Hunter 60-60-58
1863 Prestwick (£10)
168 Willie Park 56-54-58 (£6)
170 Tom Morris Snr 56-58-56
172 David Park 55-63-54
1864 Prestwick
167 Tom Morris Snr 54-58-55
169 Andrew Strath 56-57-56
175 Robert Andrew 57-58-60
1865 Prestwick
162 Andrew Strath 55-54-53
164 Willie Park 56-52-56
171 William Dow
1866 Prestwick
169 Willie Park 54-56-59
171 David Park 58-57-56
176 Robert Andrew 58-59-59
1867 Prestwick
170 Tom Morris Snr 58-54-58
172 Willie Park 58-56-58
174 Andrew Strath 61-57-56
1868 Prestwick
157 Tom Morris Jnr 50-55-52
159 Robert Andrew 53-54-52
162 Willie Park 58-50-54
1869 Prestwick
154 Tom Morris Jnr 51-54-49
157 Tom Morris Snr 54-50-53
165 S Mure Fergusson* 57-54-54
1870 Prestwick
149 Tom Morris Jnr 47-51-51
161 Bob Kirk 52-52-57
David Strath 54-49-58
1871 No competition
1872 Prestwick
166 Tom Morris Jnr 57-56-53
169 David Strath 56-52-61
177 William Doleman* 63-60-54
1873 St Andrews
179 Tom Kidd 91-88
180 Jamie Anderson 91-89
183 Tom Morris Jnr 94-89
Bob Kirk 91-92
1874 Musselburgh
159 Mungo Park 75-84
161 Tom Morris Jnr 83-78
162 George Paxton 80-82
1875 Prestwick
166 Willie Park 56-59-51
168 Bob Martin 56-58-54
171 Mungo Park 59-57-55
1876 St Andrews
176 Bob Martin 86-90
David Strath 86-90
183 Willie Park

Martin declared winner when Strath refused to play-off.

1877 Musselburgh
160 Jamie Anderson 40-42-37-41
162 Bob Pringle 44-38-40-40
164 Bob Ferguson 40-40-40-44
William Cosgrove 41-39-44-40

1878 Prestwick
157 Jamie Anderson 53-53-51
159 Bob Kirk 53-55-51
161 JOF Morris 50-56-55

1879 St Andrews
169 Jamie Anderson 84-85
172 James Allan 88-84
Andrew Kirkaldy 86-86

1880 Musselburgh (£20)
162 Bob Ferguson 81-81 (£8)
167 Peter Paxton 81-86
168 Ned Cosgrove 82-86

1881 Prestwick
170 Bob Ferguson 53-60-57
173 Jamie Anderson 57-60-56
177 Ned Cosgrove 61-59-57

1882 St Andrews
171 Bob Ferguson 83-88
174 Willie Fernie 88-86
175 Jamie Anderson 87-88
John Kirkaldy 86-89
Bob Martin 89-86
Fitz Boothby* 86-89

1883 Musselburgh
159 Willie Fernie 75-84
159 Bob Ferguson 79-80
160 W Brown 83-77
Fernie won play-off 158 (81-77); Ferguson 159 (82-77)

1884 Prestwick
160 Jack Simpson 78-82
164 David Rollan 81-83
Willie Fernie 80-84

1885 St Andrews
171 Bob Martin 84-87
172 Archie Simpson 83-89
173 David Ayton 89-84

1886 Musselburgh
157 David Brown 79-78
159 Willie Campbell 78-81
160 Ben Campbell 79-81

1887 Prestwick
161 Willie Park Jnr 82-79
162 Bob Martin 81-81
164 Willie Campbell 77-87

1888 St Andrews
171 Jack Burns 86-85
172 David Anderson Jnr 86-86
Ben Sayers 85-87

1889 Musselburgh
155 Willie Park Jnr 39-39-39-38
Andrew Kirkaldy 39-38-39-39
159 Bernard Sayers 39-40-41-39
Park won play-off 158 (82-76); Kirkaldy 163 (85-78)

1890 Prestwick
164 John Ball* 82-82
167 Willie Fernie 85-82
A Simpson 85-82

1891 St Andrews
166 Hugh Kirkaldy 83-83
168 Willie Fernie 84-84
Andrew Kirkaldy 84-84

1892 Muirfield
305 Harold Hilton* 78-81-72-74
308 John Ball* 75-80-74-79
James Kirkaldy 77-83-73-75
Alex Herd 77-78-77-76

1893 Prestwick (£100)
322 Willie Auchterlonie (£30) 78-81-81-82
324 Johnny Laidlay* 80-83-80-81
325 Alex Herd 82-81-78-84

1894 Sandwich
326 JH Taylor 84-80-81-81
331 Douglas Rolland 86-79-84-82
332 Andrew Kirkaldy 86-79-83-84

1895 St Andrews
322 JH Taylor 86-78-80-78
326 Alex Herd 82-77-82-85
332 Andrew Kirkaldy 81-83-84-84

1896 Muirfield
316 Harry Vardon 83-78-78-77
JH Taylor 77-78-81-80
319 Freddie Tait* 83-75-84-77
Vardon won play-off 157; Taylor 156

1897 Hoylake
314 Harold Hilton* 80-75-84-75
315 James Braid 80-74-82-79
317 Freddie Tait* 79-79-80-79
G. Pulford 80-79-79-79

1898 Prestwick
307 Harry Vardon 79-75-77-76
308 Willie Park Jnr 76-75-78-79
309 Harold Hilton* 76-81-77-75

1899 Sandwich
310 Harry Vardon 76-76-81-77
315 Jack White 79-79-82-75
319 Andrew Kirkaldy 81-79-82-77

1900 St Andrews (£115)
309 JH Taylor 79-77-78-75 (£50)
317 Harry Vardon 79-81-80-77
322 James Braid 82-81-80-79

1901 Muirfield
309 James Braid 79-76-74-80
312 Harry Vardon 77-78-79-78
313 JH Taylor 79-83-74-77

1902 Hoylake
307 Alex Herd 77-76-73-81
308 Harry Vardon 72-77-80-79
James Braid 78-76-80-74

1903 Prestwick
300 Harry Vardon 73-77-72-78
306 Tom Vardon 76-81-75-74
308 Jack White 77-78-74-79

1904 Sandwich
296 Jack White 80-75-72-69
297 James Braid 77-80-69-71
JH Taylor 77-78-74-68

1905 St Andrews
318 James Braid 81-78-78-81
323 JH Taylor 80-85-78-80
R Jones 81-77-87-78

1906 Muirfield
300 James Braid 77-76-74-73
304 JH Taylor 77-72-75-80
305 Harry Vardon 77-73-77-78

1907 Hoylake
312 Arnaud Massy (France) 76-81-78-77
314 JH Taylor 79-79-76-80
317 Tom Vardon 81-81-80-75
G Pulford 81-78-80-78

1908 Prestwick
291 James Braid 70-72-77-72
299 Tom Ball 76-73-76-74
301 Ted Ray 79-71-75-76

1909 Deal
295 JH Taylor 74-73-74-74
301 James Braid 79-75-73-74
Tom Ball 74-75-76-76

1910 St Andrews (£125)
299 James Braid 76-73-74-76 (£50)
303 Alex Herd 78-74-75-76
304 George Duncan 73-77-71-83

1911 Sandwich
303 Harry Vardon 74-74-75-80
Arnaud Massy (France) 75-78-74-76
304 Harold Hilton 76-74-78-76
Vardon won play-off; Massy conceded after 35th hole

1912 Muirfield
295 Ted Ray 71-73-76-75
299 Harry Vardon 75-72-81-71
303 James Braid 77-71-77-78

1913 Hoylake
304 JH Taylor 73-75-77-79
312 Ted Ray 73-74-81-84
313 Harry Vardon 79-75-79-80
Michael Moran (Ireland) 76-74-89-74

1914 Prestwick
306 Harry Vardon 73-77-78-78
309 JH Taylor 74-78-74-83
310 HB Simpson 77-80-78-75

1920 Deal (£225)
303 George Duncan (£75) 80-80-71-72
305 Alex Herd 72-81-77-75
306 Ted Ray 72-83-78-73

1921 St Andrews
296 Jock Hutchison (US) 72-75-79-70
Roger Wethered 78-75-72-71
298 Tom Kerrigan (US) 74-80-72-72
Hutchison won play-off 150 (74-76); Wethered 159 (77-82)

1922 Sandwich
300 Walter Hagan (US) 76-73-79-72
301 George Duncan 76-75-81-69
Jim Barnes (US) 75-76-77-73

1923 Troon
295 Arthur Havers 73-73-73-76
296 Walter Hagen (US) 76-71-74-75
297 Macdonald Smith (US) 80-73-69-75

1924 Hoylake
301 Walter Hagen (US) 77-73-74-77
302 Ernest Whitcombe 77-70-77-78
304 Macdonald Smith (US) 76-74-77-77
Frank Ball 78-75-74-77

1925 Prestwick
300 Jim Barnes (US) 70-77-79-74
301 Archie Compston 76-75-75-75
Ted Ray 77-76-75-73

1926 Royal Lytham
291 Bobby Jones Jnr* (US) 72-72-73-74
293 Al Watrous (US) 71-75-69-78
295 Walter Hagen (US) 68-77-74-76
George Von Elm (US) 75-72-76-72

1927 St Andrews (£275)
285 Bobby Jones Jnr (US) 68-72-73-72 (£100)
291 Aubrey Boomer 76-70-73-72
Fred Robson 76-72-69-74

1928 Sandwich
292 Walter Hagen (US) 75-73-72-72
294 Gene Sarazen (US) 72-76-73-73
295 Archie Compston 75-74-73-73

1929 Muirfield
292 Walter Hagen (US) 75-67-75-75
298 John Farrell (US) 72-75-76-75
299 Leo Diegel (US) 71-69-82-77

1930 Hoylake (£400)
291 Bobby Jones Jnr* (US) 70-72-74-75 (£100)
293 Leo Diegel (US) 74-73-71-75
Macdonald Smith (US) 70-77-75-71

1931 Carnoustie
296 Tommy Armour (US) 73-75-77-71
297 Jose Jurado (Argentina) 76-71-73-77
298 Percy Alliss 74-78-73-73
Gene Sarazen (US) 74-76-75-73

1932 Prince's
283 Gene Sarazen (US) 70-69-70-74
288 Macdonald Smith (US) 71-76-71-70
289 Arthur Havers 74-71-68-76

1933 St Andrews
292 Densmore Shute (US) 73-73-73-73
Craig Wood (US) 77-72-68-75
293 Sid Easterbrook 73-72-71-77
Gene Sarazen (US) 72-73-73-75
Leo Diegel (US) 75-70-71-77
Shute won play-off 149 (75-74); Wood 154 (78-76)

1934 Sandwich
283 Henry Cotton 67-65-72-79
288 Sid Brews 76-71-70-71
290 Alf Padgham 71-70-75-74

1935 Muirfield
283 Alf Perry 69-75-67-72
287 Alf Padgham 70-72-74-71
288 Charles Whitcombe 71-68-73-76

1936 Hoylake
287 Alf Padgham 73-72-71-71
288 Jimmy Adams 71-73-71-73
289 Henry Cotton 73-72-70-74
Marcel Dallemagne (France) 73-72-75-69

1937 Carnoustie
290 Henry Cotton 74-72-73-71
292 Reg Whitcombe 72-70-74-76
293 Charles Lacey (US) 76-75-70-72

1938 Sandwich
295 Reg Whitcombe 71-71-75-78
297 Jimmy Adams 70-71-78-78
298 Henry Cotton 74-73-77-74

1939 St Andrews (£500)
290 Dick Burton 70-72-77-71 (£100)
292 Johnny Bulla (US) 77-71-71-73
294 Johnny Fallon 71-73-71-79
Sam King 74-72-75-73
Reg Whitcombe 71-75-74-74
Alf Perry 71-74-73-76
Bill Shankland (Australia) 72-73-72-77

1946 St Andrews (£1,000)
290 Sam Snead (US) 71-70-74-75 (£150)
294 Bobby Locke (S Africa) 69-74-75-76
Johnny Bulla (US) 71-72-72-79

1947 Hoylake
293 Fred Daly 73-70-78-72
294 Reg Horne 77-74-72-71
Frank Stranahan* (US) 71-79-72-72

1948 Muirfield
284 Henry Cotton 71-66-75-72
289 Fred Daly 72-71-73-73
290 Norman von Nida (Australia) 71-72-76-71
Jack Hargreaves 76-68-73-73
Charlie Ward 69-72-75-74
Roberto de Vicenzo (Argentina) 70-73-72-75

1949 Sandwich
283 Bobby Lock (S Africa) 69-76-68-70
Harry Bradshaw (Eire) 68-77-68-70
285 Roberto de Vicenzo (Argentina) 68-75-73-69
Locke won play-off 135 (67-68); Bradshaw 147 (74-73)

1950 Troon (£1,700)
279 Bobby Locke(S Africa) 69-72-70-68 (£300)
281 Roberto de Vicenzo (Argentina) 72-71-68-70
282 Fred Daly 75-72-69-66
Dai Rees 71-68-72-71

1951 Royal Portrush
285 Max Faulkner 71-70-70-74
287 Tony Cerda (Argentina) 74-72-71-70
290 Charlie Ward 75-73-74-68

1952 Royal Lytham
287 Bobby Locke (S Africa) 69-71-74-73
288 Peter Thomson (Australia) 68-73-77-70
289 Fred Daly 67-69-77-76

1953 Carnoustie
282 Ben Hogan (US) 73-71-70-68
286 Frank Stranahan* (US) 70-74-73-69
Dai Rees 72-70-73-71
Peter Thomson (Australia) 72-72-71-71
Antonio Cerda (Argentina) 75-71-69-71

1954 Royal Birkdale
283 Peter Thomson (Australia) 72-71-69-71
284 Sid Scott 76-67-69-72
Dai Rees 72-71-69-72
Bobby Locke (S Africa) 74-71-69-70

1955 St Andrews (£3,750)
281 Peter Thomson (Australia) 71-68-70-72 (£1,000)
283 Johnny Fallon 73-67-73-70
284 Frank Jowle 70-71-69-74

1956 Hoylake
286 Peter Thomson (Australia) 70-70-72-74
289 Flory van Donck (Belgium) 71-74-70-74
290 Roberto de Vicenzo (Argentina) 71-70-79-70

1957 St Andrews
279 Bobby Locke (S Africa) 69-72-68-70
282 Peter Thomson (Australia) 73-69-70 70
283 Eric Brown 67-72-73-71

1958 Royal Lytham
278 Peter Thomson (Australia) 66-72-67-73
David Thomas 70-68-69-71
279 Eric Brown 73-70-65-71
Christy O'Connor (Eire) 67-68-73-71
Thomson won play-off 139 (68-71); Thomas 143 (69-74)

1959 Muirfield
284 Gary Player (S Africa) 75-71-70-68
286 Flory van Donck (Belgium) 70-70-73-73
Fred Bullock 68-70-74-74

1960 St Andrews (£7,000)
278 Kel Nagle (Australia) 69-67-71-71 (£1,250)
279 Arnold Palmer (US) 70-71-70-68
282 Bernard Hunt 72-73-71-66
Harold Henning (S Africa) 72-72-69-69
Roberto de Vicenzo (Argentina) 67-67-75-73

1961 Royal Birkdale
284 Arnold Palmer (US) 70-73-69-72
285 Dai Rees 68-74-71-72
288 Christy O'Connor (Eire) 71-77-67-73
Neil Coles 70-77-69-72

1962 Troon
276 Arnold Palmer (US) 71-69-67-69
282 Kel Nagle (Australia) 71-71-70-70
289 Brian Huggett 75-71-74-69
Phil Rodgers (US) 75-70-72-72

1963 Royal Lytham
277 Bob Charles (NZ) 68-72-66-71
Phil Rodgers (US) 67-68-73-69
278 Jack Nicklaus (US) 71-67-70-70
Charles won play-off 140 (69-71); Rodgers 148 (72-76)

1964 St Andrews (£8,500)
279 Tony Lema (US) 73-68-68-70 (£1,500)
284 Jack Nicklaus (US) 76-74 66-68
285 Roberto de Vicenzo (Argentina) 76-72-70-67

1965 Royal Birkdale
285 Peter Thomson (Australia) 74-68-72-71
287 Christy O'Connor (Eire) 69-73-74-71
Brian Huggett 73-68-76-70

1966 Muirfield
282 Jack Nicklaus (US) 70-67-75-70
283 David Thomas 72-73-69-69
Doug Sanders (US) 71-70-72-70

1967 Hoylake (£15,000)
278 Roberto de Vicenzo (Argentina) 70-71-67-70 (£2,100)
280 Jack Nicklaus (US) 71-69-71-69
284 Clive Clark 70-73-69-72
Gary Player (S Africa) 72-71-67-74

1968 Carnoustie
289 Gary Player (S Africa) 74-71-71-73
291 Jack Nicklaus (US) 76-69-73-73
Bob Charles (NZ) 72-72-71-76

1969 Royal Lytham
280 Tony Jacklin 68-70-70-72
282 Bob Charles (NZ) 66-69-75-72
283 Peter Thomson (Australia) 71-70-70-72
Roberto de Vicenzo (Argentina) 72-73-66-72

1970 St Andrews (£40,000)
283 Jack Nicklaus (US) 68-69-73-73 (£5,250)
Doug Sanders (US) 68-71-71-73
285 Harold Henning (S Africa) 67-72-73-73
Lee Trevino (US) 68-68-72-77
Nicklaus won play-off 72; Sanders 73

1971 Royal Birkdale
278 Lee Trevino (US) 69-70-69-70
279 Lu Liang Huan (Formosa) 70-70-69-70
280 Tony Jacklin 69-70-70-71

1972 Muirfield
278 Lee Trevino (US) 71-70-66-71
279 Jack Nicklaus (US) 70-72-71-66
280 Tony Jacklin (US) 69-72-67-72

1973 Troon (£50,000)
276 Tom Weiskopf (US) 68-67-71-70 (£5,500)
279 Neil Coles 71-72-70-66
Johnny Miller (US) 70-68-69-72

1974 Royal Lytham
282 Gary Player (S Africa) 69-68-75-70
286 Peter Oosterhuis 71-71-73-71
287 Jack Nicklaus (US) 74-72-70-71

1975 Carnoustie (£75,000)
279 Tom Watson (US) 71-67-69-72 (£7,500)
Jack Newton (Australia) 69-71-65-74
280 Bobby Cole (S Africa) 72-66-66-76
Jack Nicklaus (US) 69-71-68-72
Johnny Miller (US) 71-69-66-74
Watson won play-off 71; Newton 72

1976 Royal Birkdale
279 Johnny Miller (US) 72-68-73-66
285 Jack Nicklaus (US) 74-70-72-69
Severiano Ballesteros (Spain) 69-69-73-74

1977 Turnberry (£100,000)
268 Tom Watson (US) 68-70-65-65 (£10,000)
269 Jack Nicklaus (US) 68-70-65-66
279 Hubert Green (US) 72-66-74-67

1978 St Andrews (£125,000)
281 Jack Nicklaus (US) 71-72-69-69 (£12,500)
283 Simon Owen (NZ) 70-75-67-71
Ben Crenshaw (US) 70-69-73-71
Tom Kite (US) 72-69-72-70
Ray Floyd (US) 69-75-71-68

1979 Royal Lytham (£155,000)
283 Severiano Ballesteros (Spain)

73-65-75-70 (£15,000)
286 Jack Nicklaus (US)
72-69-73-72
Ben Crenshaw (US)
72-71-72-71

1980 Muirfield (£200,000)
271 Tom Watson (US)
68-70-64-69 (£25,000)
275 Lee Trevino (US)
68-67-71-69
277 Ben Crenshaw (US)
70-70-68-69

1981 Sandwich
276 Bill Rogers (US)
72-66-67-71
280 Bernhard Langer
(W Germany)
73-67-70-70
283 Mark James 72-70-68-73
Ray Floyd (US)
74-70-69-70

1982 Royal Troon (£250,000)
284 Tom Watson (US)
69-71-74-70 (£32,000)
285 Peter Oosterhuis
74-67-74-70
Nick Price
(S Africa) 69-69-74-73

1983 Royal Birkdale
(£310,000)
275 Tom Watson (US)
67-68-70-70 (£40,000)
276 Hale Irwin (US)
69-68-72-67
Andy Bean (US)
70-69-70-67

UNITED STATES OPEN CHAMPIONSHIP

Players from the US unless otherwise stated. * amateur

1895 Newport, Rhode Island
($335)
173 Horace Rawlins
45-46-41-41 ($150)
175 Willie Dunn 43-46-44-42
176 James Foulis 46-43-44-43
AW Smith* 47-43-44-42

1896 Shinnecock Hills, NY
152 James Foulis 78-74
155 Horace Rawlins 79-76
158 G Douglas 79-79

1897 Chicago, Illinois
162 Joe Lloyd 83-79
163 Willie Anderson 79-84
168 James Foulis 80-88

1898 Myopia Hunt Club, Mass
328 Fred Herd 84-85-75-84
335 Alex Smith 78-86-86-85
336 Willie Anderson
81-82-87-86

1899 Baltimore, Maryland
($750)
315 Willie Smith
77-82-79-77 ($150)
326 George Low 82-79-89-76
Val Fitzjohn 85-80-79-82
WH Way 80-85-80-81

1900 Chicago, Illinois
313 Harry Vardon (GB)
79-78-76-80
315 JH Taylor (GB)
76-82-79-78
322 David Bell 78-83-83-78

1901 Myopia Hunt Club, Mass
331 Willie Anderson
84-83-83-81 ($200)
Alex Smith 82-82-87-80
333 Willie Smith 84-86-82-81
Anderson won play-off 85, Smith 86

1902 Garden City, NY ($970)
307 Laurie Auchterlonie (GB)
78-78-74-77 ($200)
313 Stewart Gardner
82-76-77-78
Walter Travis*
82-82-75-74

1903 Baltusrol, New Jersey
307 Willie Anderson 149-79-82
David Brown 156-75-76
315 Stewart Gardner
154-82-79
Anderson won play-off 82; Brown 84

1904 Glen View, Illinois
303 Willie Anderson 75-78-78-72
308 Gilbert Nicholls 80-76-79-73
309 Fred Mackenzie 76-79-74-80

1905 Myopia Hunt Club, Mass
314 Willie Anderson 81-80-76-77
316 Alex Smith 81-80-76-79
317 Peter Robertson 79-80-81-77
PF Barrett (Canada) 81-80-81-77

1906 Onwentsia, Illinois ($900)
295 Alex Smith 73-74-73-75 ($300)
302 Willie Smith 73-81-74-74
305 Laurie Auchterlonie (GB) 76-78-75-76
James Maiden 80-73-77-75

1907 Philadelphia, Penns
302 Alec Ross 76-74-76-76
304 Gilbert Nicholls 80-73-72-79
305 Alex Campbell 78-74-78-75

1908 Myopia Hunt Club, Mass
322 Fred McLeod 82-82-81-77
Willie Smith 77-82-85-78
327 Alex Smith 80-83-83-81
McLeod won play-off 77; Smith 83

1909 Englewood, New Jersey
290 George Sargent 75-72-72-71
294 Tom McNamara 73-69-75-77
295 Alex Smith 76-73-74-72

1910 Philadelphia, Penns
298 Alex Smith 73-73-79-73
John McDermott 74-74-75-75
Macdonald Smith 74-78-75-71
Smith won play-off 71; McDermott 73

1911 Chicago, Illinois
307 John McDermott 81-72-75-79
Mike Brady 76-77-79-75
George Simpson 76-77-79-75
McDermott won play-off 80; to 82 and 85

1912 Buffalo, NY
294 John McDermott 74-75-74-71
296 Tom McNamara 74-80-73-69
299 Alex Smith 77-70-77-75
Mike J Brady 72-75-73-79

1913 Brookline, Mass
304 Francis Ouimet* 77-74-74-79
Harry Vardon (GB) 75-72-78-79
Ted Ray (GB) 79-70-76-79
Ouimet won play-off 72, to 77 & 78

1914 Midlothian, Illinois
290 Walter Hagen 68-74-75-73
291 Charles Evans Jnr* 76-74-71-70
297 George Sargent 74-77-74-72
Fred McLeod 78-73-75-71

1915 Baltusrol, New Jersey
297 Jerome Travers* 148-73-76
298 Tom McNamara 149-74-75
300 Robert MacDonald 149-73-78

1916 Minikahda, Minnesota
286 Charles Evans* 70-69-74-73
288 Jock Hutchison 73-75-72-68
290 Jim Barnes 71-74-71-74

1917-18 No championship

1919 Brae Burn, Mass ($1,300)
301 Walter Hagen 78-73-75-75 ($500)
Mike Brady 74-74-73-80
306 Jock Hutchison 78-76-76-76
Hagen won play-off 77; Brady 78

1920 Inverness, Ohio ($1,745)
295 Ted Ray (GB) 74-73-73-75 ($500)

296 Harry Vardon (GB)
74-73-71-78
Jack Burke 75-77-72-72
Leo Diegel 72-74-73-77
Jock Hutchison
69-76-74-77

1921 Columbia, Maryland
289 Jim Barnes 69-75-73-72
298 Walter Hagen 79-73-72-74
Fred McLeod 74-74-76-74

1922 Skokie, Illinois
288 Gene Sarazen 72-73-75-68
289 John Black 71-71-75-72
Bobby Jones*
74-72-70-73

1923 Inwood, New York
296 Bobby Jones*
71-73-76-76
Bobby Cruickshank
73-72-78-73
302 Jock Hutchison
70-72-82-78
Jones won play-off 76;
Cruickshank 75

1924 Oakland Hills, Michigan
297 Cyril Walker 74-74-74-75
300 Bobby Jones*
74-73-75-78
301 Bill Mehlhorn 72-75-76-78

1925 Worcester, Mass ($2,145)
291 Willie Macfarlane
74-67-72-78 ($500)
Bobby Jones*
77-70-70-74
292 Johnny Farrell
71-74-69-78
Francis Ouimet*
70-73-73-76
McFarlane won play-off 147;
Jones 148

1926 Scioto, Ohio
293 Bobby Jones*
70-79-71-73
294 Joe Turnesa 71-74-72-77
297 Bill Mehlhorn 68-75-76-78
Gene Sarazen 78-77-72-70
Leo Diegel 72-76-75-74
Johnny Farrell 76-79-69-73

1927 Oakmont, Penns
301 Tommy Armour
78-71-76-76
Harry Cooper 74-76-74-77
302 Gene Sarazen 74-74-80-74
Armour won play-off 76;
Cooper 79

1928 Olympia Fields, Illinois
($5,000)
294 Johnny Farrell
77-74-71-72 ($1,000)
Bobby Jones*
73-71-73-77
295 Roland Hancock
74-77-72-72
Farrell won play-off 143;
Jones 144

1929 Winged Foot, NY
294 Bobby Jones*
69-75-71-79
Al Espinosa 70-72-77-75
296 Gene Sarazen 71-71-76-78
Densmore Shute
73-71-76-76
Jones won play-off 141;
Espinosa 164

1930 Interlachen, Minnesota
287 Bobby Jones*
71-73-68-75
289 Macdonald Smith
70-75-74-70
292 Horton Smith 72-70-76-74

1931 Inverness, Ohio
292 Billy Burke 73-72-74-73
George von Elm
75-69-73-75
294 Leo Diegel 75-73-74-72
Burke won play-off 149-149;
von Elm 148-149

1932 Fresh Meadow, NY
($4,950)
286 Gene Sarazen
74-76-70-66 ($1,000)
289 Bobby Cruickshank
78-74-69-68
Phil Perkins 76-69-74-70

1933 North Shore, Illinois
($4,990)
287 Johnny Goodman*
75-66-70-76
288 Ralph Guldahl
76-71-70-71 ($1,000)
290 Craig Wood 73-74-71-72

1934 Merion, Penns ($5,000)
293 Olin Dutra
76-74-71-72 ($1,000)
294 Gene Sarazen 73-72-73-76
295 Wiffy Cox 71-75-74-75
Bobby Cruickshank
71-71-77-76
Harry Cooper 76-74-74-71
1935 Oakmont, Penns
299 Sam Parks Jnr
77-73-73-76
301 Jimmy Thomson
73-73-77-78
302 Walter Hagen 77-76-73-76
1936 Baltusrol, New Jersey
282 Tony Manero 73-69-73-67
284 Harry Cooper 71-70-70-73
287 Clarence Clark
69-75-71-72
1937 Oakland Hills, Michigan
($6,000)
281 Ralph Guldahl
71-69-72-69 ($1,000)
283 Sam Snead 69-73-70-71
285 Bobby Cruickshank
73-73-67-72
1938 Cherry Hills, Colorado
284 Ralph Guldahl 74-70-71-69
290 Dick Metz 73-68-70-79
292 Harry Cooper 76-69-76-71
Tony Penna 78-72-74-68
1939 Philadelphia, Penns
284 Byron Nelson 72-73-71-68
Craig Wood 70-71-71-72
Densmore Shute
70-72-70-72
Nelson won play-off 138;
Wood 141; Shute eliminated
1940 Canterbury, Ohio
287 Lawson Little 72-69-73-73
Gene Sarazen 71-74-70-72
288 Horton Smith 69-72-78-69
Little won play-off 70;
Sarazen 73
1941 Colonial Club, Texas
284 Craig Wood 73-71-70-70
287 Densmore Shute
69-75-72-71
289 Johnny Bulla 75-71-72-71
Ben Hogan 74-77-68-70
1942-45 No championships

1946 Canterbury, Ohio
($8,000)
284 Lloyd Mangrum
74-70-68-72 ($1,500)
Byron Nelson 71-71-69-73
Vic Ghezzi 71-69-72-72
Mangrum won play-off
72/72, 72/73, 72/73
1947 St Louis, Missouri
($10,000)
282 Lew Worsham
70-70-71-71 ($2,000)
Sam Snead 72-70-70-70
285 Bobby Locke
(S Africa) 68-74-70-73
Porky Oliver 73-70-71-71
Worsham won play-off 69;
Snead 70
1948 Riviera California
276 Ben Hogan 67-72-68-69
278 Jimmy Demaret
71-70-68-69
280 Jim Turnesa 71-69-70-70
1949 Medinah, Illinois
286 Cary Middlecoff
75-67-69-75
287 Clayton Heafner
72-71-71-73
Sam Snead 73-73-71-70
1950 Merion, Penns ($14,900)
287 Ben Hogan
72-69-72-74 ($4,000)
Lloyd Mangrum
72-70-69-76
George Fazio 73-72-72-70
Hogan won play-off 69, to
73 and 75
1951 Oakland Hills, Michigan
($14,800)
287 Ben Hogan
76-73-71-67 ($4,000)
289 Clayton Heafner
72-75-73-69
291 Bobby Locke
(S Africa) 73-71-74-73
1952 Northwood, Texas
($14,900)
281 Julius Boros
71-71-68-71 ($4,000)
285 Porky Oliver 71-72-70-72
286 Ben Hogan 69-69-74-74

1953 Oakmont, Penns ($20,400)
283 Ben Hogan
67-72-73-71 ($5,000)
289 Sam Snead 72-69-72-76
292 Lloyd Mangrum
73-70-74-75

1954 Baltusrol, New Jersey ($23,280)
284 Ed Furgol
71-70-71-72 ($6,000)
285 Gene Littler 70-69-76-70
286 Dick Mayer 72-71-70-73
Lloyd Mangrum
72-71-72-71

1955 Olympic, California ($25,480)
287 Jack Fleck
76-69-75-67 ($6,000)
Ben Hogan 72-73-72-70
292 Sam Snead 79-69-70-74
Tommy Bolt 67-77-75-73
Fleck won play-off 69; Hogan 72

1956 Oak Hill, NY ($24,000)
281 Cary Middlecoff
71-70-70-70 ($6,000)
282 Julius Boros 71-71-71-69
Ben Hogan 72-68-72-70

1957 Inverness, Ohio ($28,560)
282 Dick Mayer
70-68-74-70 ($7,200)
Cary Middlecoff
71-75-68-68
283 Jimmy Demaret
68-73-70-72
Mayer won play-off 72, Middlecoff 79

1958 Southern Hills, Oklahoma ($35,000)
283 Tommy Bolt
71-71-69-72 ($8,000)
287 Gary Player
(S Africa) 75-68-73-71
289 Julius Boros 71-75-72-71

1959 Winged Foot, NY ($49,200)
282 Billy Casper Jnr
71-68-69-74 ($12,000)
283 Bob Rosburg 75-70-67-71
284 Claude Harmon 72-71-70-71
Mike Souchak 71-70-72-71

1960 Cherry Hills, Colorado ($62,020)
280 Arnold Palmer
72-71-72-65 ($14,400)
282 Jack Nicklaus*
71-71-69-71
283 Dutch Harrison
74-70-70-69
Julius Boros 73-69-68-73

1961 Oakland Hills, Michigan ($68,300)
281 Gene Littler
73-68-72-68 ($14,000)
282 Bob Goalby 70-72-69-71
Doug Sanders 72-67-71-72

1962 Oakmont, Penns ($81,600)
283 Jack Nicklaus
72-70-72-69 ($17,500)
Arnold Palmer
71-68-73-71
285 Phil Rodgers 74-70-69-72
Bobby Nichols
70-72-70-73
Nicklaus won play-off 71; Palmer 74

1963 Brookline, Mass ($96,350)
293 Julius Boros
71-74-76-72 ($17,500)
Jacky Cupit 70-72-76-75
Arnold Palmer
73-69-77-74
Boros won play-off 70, to 73 & 76

1964 Congressional, Washington DC ($95,400)
278 Ken Venturi
72-70-66-70 ($17,000)
282 Tommy Jacobs
72-64-70-76
283 Bob Charles 72-72-71-68

1965 Bellerive, Missouri ($131,690)
282 Gary Player (S Africa)
70-70-71-71 ($26,000)
Kel Nagle
(Australia) 68-73-72-69
284 Frank Beard 74-69-70-71
Player won play-off 71; Nagle 74

1966 Olympic, California
($155,290)
278 Billy Casper
69-68-73-68 ($26,500)
Arnold Palmer 71-66-70-71
285 Jack Nicklaus 71-71-69-74
Casper won play-off 69;
Palmer 73

1967 Baltusrol, New Jersey
($177,800)
275 Jack Nicklaus
71-67-72-65 ($30,000)
279 Arnold Palmer
69-68-73-69
281 Don January 69-72-70-70

1968 Oak Hill, NY ($188,800)
275 Lee Trevino
69-68-69-69 ($30,000)
279 Jack Nicklaus 72-70-70-67
281 Bert Yancey 67-68-70-76

1969 Champions, Texas
($205,300)
281 Orville Moody
71-70-68-72 ($30,000)
282 Deane Beman 68-69-73-72
Al Geiberger 68-72-72-70
Bob Rosburg 70-69-72-71

1970 Hazeltine, Minnesota
($203,500)
281 Tony Jacklin (GB)
71-70-70-70 ($30,000)
288 Dave Hill 75-69-71-73
289 Bob Lunn 77-72-70-70
Bob Charles (NZ)
76-71-75-67

1971 Merion, Penns ($200,000)
280 Lee Trevino
70-72-69-69 ($30,000)
Jack Nicklaus 69-72-68-71
282 Bob Rosburg 71-72-70-69
Jim Colbert 69-69-75-71
Trevino won play-off, 68;
Nicklaus 71

1972 Pebble Beach, California
($202,400)
290 Jack Nicklaus
71-73-72-74 ($30,000)
293 Bruce Crampton
(Australia) 74-70-73-76
294 Arnold Palmer
77-68-73-76

1973 Oakmont, Penns
($227,200)
279 Johnny Miller
71-69-76-63 ($35,000)
280 John Schlee 73-70-67-70
281 Tom Weiskopf
73-69-69-70

1974 Winged Foot, NY
($227,700)
287 Hale Irwin
73-70-71-73 ($35,000)
289 Forest Fezler 75-70-74-70
290 Lou Graham 71-75-74-70
Bert Yancey 76-69-73-72

1975 Medinah, Illinois
($244,000)
287 Lou Graham
74-72-68-73 ($40,000)
John Mahaffey Jnr
73-71-72-71
288 Bob Murphy 74-73-72-69
Hale Irwin 74-71-73-70
Ben Crenshaw 70-68-76-74
Frank Beard 74-69-67-78
Graham won play-off, 71;
Mahaffey 73

1976 Atlanta, Georgia
($268,000)
277 Jerry Pate
71-69-69-68 ($42,000)
279 Al Geiberger 70-69-71-69
Tom Weiskopf 73-70-68-68

1977 Southern Hills, Oklahoma
($284,990)
278 Hubert Green
69-67-72-70 ($45,000)
279 Lou Graham 72-71-68-68
281 Tom Weiskopf
71-71-68-71

1978 Cherry Hills, Colorado
($310,200)
285 Andy North
70-70-71-74 ($45,000)
286 Jesse Snead 70-72-72-72
Dave Stockton 71-73-70-72

1979 Inverness, Ohio ($330,400)
284 Hale Irwin
74-68-67-75 ($50,000)
286 Jerry Pate 71-74-69-72
Gary Player
(S Africa) 73-73-72-68

1980 Baltusrol, New Jersey ($356,700)
272 Jack Nicklaus 63-71-70-68 ($55,000)
274 Isao Aoki (Japan) 68-68-68-70
276 Keith Fergus 66-70-70-70
Tom Watson 71-68-67-70
Lon Hinkle 66-70-69-71

1981 Merion, Penns ($361,730)
273 David Graham (Australia) 68-68-70-67 ($55,000)
276 Bill Rogers 70-68-69-69
George Burns 69-66-68-73

1982 Pebble Beach, California ($385,000)
282 Tom Watson 72-72-68-70 ($60,000)
284 Jack Nicklaus 74-70-71-69
286 Bobby Clampett 71-73-72-70
Dan Pohl 72-74-70-70

1983 Oakmont, Penns ($506,184)
280 Larry Nelson 75-73-65-67 ($72,000)
281 Tom Watson 72-70-70-69
283 Gil Morgan 73-72-70-68

THE MASTERS TOURNAMENT

Augusta National

Players from the US unless otherwise stated * amateur

1934 ($5,000)
284 Horton Smith 70-72-70-72 ($1,500)
285 Craig Wood 71-74-69-71
286 Billy Burke 72-71-70-73
Paul Runyan 74-71-70-71

1935
282 Gene Sarazen 68-71-73-70
Craig Wood 69-72-68-73
284 Olin Dutra 70-70-70-74
Sarazen won play-off 144-149

1936
285 Horton Smith 74-71-68-72
286 Harry Cooper 70-69-71-76
287 Gene Sarazen 78-67-72-70

1937
283 Byron Nelson 66-72-75-70
285 Ralph Guldahl 69-72-68-76
286 Ed Dudley 70-71-71-74

1938
285 Henry Picard 71-72-72-70
287 Ralph Guldahl 73-70-73-71
Harry Cooper 68-77-71-71

1939
279 Ralph Guldahl 72-68-70-69
280 Sam Snead 70-70-72-68
282 Billy Burke 69-72-71-70
Lawson Little 72-72-68-70

1940
280 Jimmy Demaret 67-72-70-71
284 Lloyd Mangrum 64-75-71-74
285 Byron Nelson 69-72-74-70

1941
280 Craig Wood 66-71-71-72
283 Byron Nelson 71-69-73-70
285 Sam Byrd 73-70-68-74

1942
280 Byron Nelson 68-67-72-73
Ben Hogan 73-70-67-70
283 Paul Runyan 67-73-72-71
Nelson won play-off, 69; Hogan 70

1946 ($10,000)
282 Herman Keiser 69-68-71-74 ($2,500)
283 Ben Hogan 74-70-69-70
287 Bob Hamilton 75-69-71-72

1947
281 Jimmy Demaret 69-71-70-71
283 Byron Nelson 69-72-72-70
Frank Stranahan 73-72-70-68

1948
279 Claude Harmon
70-70-69-70
284 Cary Middlecoff
74-71-69-70
287 Chick Harbert 71-70-70-76
1949
282 Sam Snead
73-75-67-67 ($2,750)
285 Johnny Bulla 74-73-69-69
Lloyd Mangrum
69-74-72-70
1950 ($12,000)
283 Jimmy Demaret
70-72-72-69 ($2,800)
285 Jim Ferrier 70-67-73-75
287 Sam Snead 71-74-70-72
1951 ($18,450)
280 Ben Hogan
70-72-70-68 ($3,000)
282 Skee Riegel 73-68-70-71
286 Lloyd Mangrum
69-74-70-73
Lew Worsham
71-71-72-72
1952 ($24,600)
286 Sam Snead
70-67-77-72 ($4,000)
290 Jack Burke Jnr 76-67-78-69
291 Al Besselink 70-76-71-74
Tommy Bolt 71-71-75-74
Jim Ferrier 72-70-77-72
1953 ($26,800)
274 Ben Hogan 70-69-66-69
279 Porky Oliver Jnr
69-73-67-70
282 Lloyd Mangrum
74-68-71-69
1954 ($33,500)
289 Sam Snead
74-73-70-72 ($5,000)
Ben Hogan 72-73-69-75
290 Billy Joe Patton*
70-74-75-71
Snead won play-off, 70; Hogan 71
1955 ($34,250)
279 Cary Middlecoff
72-65-72-70
286 Ben Hogan 73-68-72-73
287 Sam Snead 72-71-74-70

1956 ($42,000)
289 Jack Burke Jnr
72-71-75-71 ($6,000)
290 Ken Venturi*
66-69-75-80
291 Cary Middlecoff
67-72-75-77
1957 ($53,300)
283 Doug Ford
72-73-72-66 ($8,750)
286 Sam Snead 72-68-74-72
287 Jimmy Demaret
72-70-75-70
1958 ($60,050)
284 Arnold Palmer
70-73-68-73 ($11,250)
285 Doug Ford 74-71-70-70
285 Fred Hawkins 71-75-68-71
1959 ($76,100)
284 Art Wall Jnr
73-74-71-66 ($15,000)
285 Cary Middlecoff
74-71-68-72
286 Arnold Palmer
71-70-71-74
1960 ($87,050)
282 Arnold Palmer
67-73-72-70 ($17,500)
283 Ken Venturi 73-69-71-70
284 Dow Finsterwald
71-70-72-71
1961 ($99,500)
280 Gary Player (S Africa)
69-68-69-74 ($20,000)
281 Arnold Palmer
68-69-73-71
Charlie Coe* 72-71-69-69
1962 ($109,100)
280 Arnold Palmer
70-66-69-75
Gary Player
(S Africa) 67-71-71-71
Dow Finsterwald
74-68-65-73
Palmer won play-off, 68; Player 71, Finsterwald 77
1963 ($112,500)
286 Jack Nicklaus 74-66-74-72
287 Tony Lema 74-69-74-70
288 Julius Boros 76-69-71-72
Sam Snead 70-73-74-71

1964 ($129,800)
276 Arnold Palmer
69-68-69-70
282 Dave Marr 70-73-69-70
Jack Nicklaus 71-73-71-67
1965 ($137,675)
271 Jack Nicklaus 67-71-64-69
280 Arnold Palmer
70-68-72-70
Gary Player
(S Africa) 65-73-69-73
1966 ($152,880)
288 Jack Nicklaus 68-76-72-72
Tommy Jacobs 75-71-70-72
Gay Brewer 74-72-72-70
Nicklaus won play-off, 70; Jacobs 72, Brewer 78
1967 ($163,350)
280 Gay Brewer 73-68-72-67
281 Bobby Nichols
72-69-70-70
284 Bert Yancey 67-73-71-73
1968 ($172,475)
277 Bob Goalby 70-70-71-66
278 Roberto de Vicenzo
(Argentina) 69-73-70-66
279 Bert Yancey 71-71-72-65
1969 ($186,975)
281 George Archer
67-73-69-72
282 Tom Weiskopf
71-71-69-71
George Knudson
(Canada) 70-73-69-70
Billy Casper 66-71-71-74
1970 ($194,301)
279 Billy Casper
72-68-68-71 ($25,000)
Gene Littler 69-70-70-70
280 Gary Player
(S Africa) 74-68-68-70
Casper won play-off, 69; Littler 74
1971 ($197,976)
279 Charles Coody
66-73-70-70
281 Johnny Miller 72-73-68-68
Jack Nicklaus 70-71-68-72
1972 ($204,649)
286 Jack Nicklaus 68-71-73-74
289 Tom Weiskopf 74-71-70-74
Bruce Crampton
72-75-69-73
Bobby Mitchell
73-72-71-73
1973 ($224,825)
283 Tommy Aaron
68-73-74-68 ($30,000)
284 JC Snead 70-71-73-70
285 Peter Oosterhuis
(GB) 73-70-68-74
Jack Nicklaus 69-77-73-66
Jim Jamieson 73-71-70-71
1974 ($229,549)
278 Gary Player (S Africa)
71-71-66-70 ($35,000)
280 Dave Stockton
71-66-70-73
Tom Weiskopf
71-69-70-70
1975 ($242,750)
276 Jack Nicklaus
68-67-73-68 ($40,000)
277 Johnny Miller 75-71-65-66
Tom Weiskopf
69-72-66-70
1976 ($254,852)
271 Ray Floyd 65-66-70-70
279 Ben Crenshaw
70-70-72-67
282 Jack Nicklaus 67-69-73-73
Larry Ziegler 67-71-72-72
1977 ($280,477)
276 Tom Watson 70-69-70-67
278 Jack Nicklaus 72-70-70-66
280 Tom Kite 70-73-70-67
Rik Messengale
70-73-67-70
1978 ($283,877)
277 Gary Player
(S Africa)
72-72-69-64 ($45,000)
278 Rod Funseth 73-66-70-69
Hubert Green 72-69-65-72
Tom Watson 73-68-68-69
1979 ($299,625)
280 Fuzzy Zoeller
70-71-69-70 ($50,000)
Tom Watson 68-71-70-71
Ed Sneed 68-67-69-76
Zoeller won play-off at 2nd extra hole

1980 ($359,849)
275 Severiano Ballesteros (Spain) 66-69-68-72 ($55,000)
279 Gibby Gilbert 70-74-68-67
Jack Newton 68-74-69-68

1981 ($362,587)
280 Tom Watson 71-68-70-71 ($60,000)
282 Jack Nicklaus 70-65-75-72
Johnny Miller 69-72-73-68

1982 ($368,652)
284 Craig Stadler 75-69-67-73 ($64,000)
Dan Pohl 75-75-67-67
285 Severiano Ballesteros (Spain) 73-73-68-71
Jerry Pate 74-73-67-71
Stadler won play-off at 1st extra hole

1983 ($519,699)
280 Severiano Ballesteros (Spain) 68-70-73-69 ($90,000)
284 Ben Crenshaw 76-70-70-68
Tom Kite 70-72-73-69

THE UNITED STATES PGA

Players from the US unless otherwise stated

1916 Siwanoy, NY
Jim Barnes beat Jock Hutchison 1 hole

1919 Engineers, NY
Jim Barnes beat Freddy McLeod 6 & 5

1920 Flossmoor, Illinois
Jock Hutchison beat JD Edgar 1 hole

1921 Inwood, NY
Walter Hagen beat Jim Barnes 3 & 2

1922 Oakmont, Penns
Gene Sarazen beat Emmet French 4 & 3

1923 Pelham, NY
Gene Sarazen beat Walter Hagen at 38th

1924 French Lick, Indiana
Walter Hagen beat Jim Barnes 2 holes

1925 Olympia Fields, Illinois
Walter Hagen beat Bill Mehlhorn 6 & 5

1926 Salisbury, NY
Walter Hagen beat Leo Diegel 5 & 3

1927 Cedar Crest, Texas
Walter Hagen beat Joe Turnesa 1 hole

1928 Baltimore, Maryland
Leo Diegel beat Al Espinosa 6 & 5

1929 Hillcrest, California
Leo Diegel beat John Farrell 6 & 4

1930 Fresh Meadow, NY
Tommy Armour beat Gene Sarazen 1 hole

1931 Wannamoisett, Rhode Island
Tom Creavy beat Densmore Shute 2 & 1

1932 Keller, Minnesota
Olin Dutra beat Frank Walsh 4 & 3

1933 Blue Mound, Wisconsin
Gene Sarazen beat Willie Goggin 5 & 4

1934 Park, NY
Paul Runyan beat Craig Wood at 38th

1935 Twin Hills, Oklahoma
Johnny Revolta beat Tommy Armour 5 & 4

1936 Pinehurst, N Carolina
Densmore Shute beat Jimmy Thomson 3 & 2

1937 Pittsburgh, Penns
Densmore Shute beat Harold McSpaden at 37th

1938 Shawnee, Penns
Paul Runyan beat Sam Snead 8 & 7

1939 Pomonok, NY
Henry Picard beat Byron Nelson at 37th

1940 Hershey, Penns
Byron Nelson beat Sam Snead 1 hole

1941 Cherry Hills, Colorado
Vic Ghezzi beat Byron Nelson at 38th

1942 Seaview, New Jersey
Sam Snead beat Jim Turnesa 2 & 1

1944 Manito, Washington
Bob Hamilton beat Byron Nelson 1 hole

1945 Morraine, Ohio
Byron Nelson beat Sam Byrd 4 & 3

1946 Portland, Oregon
Ben Hogan beat Porky Oliver 6 & 4

1947 Plum Hollow, Michigan
Jim Ferrier beat Chick Harbert 2 & 1

1948 Norwood Hills, Missouri
Ben Hogan beat Mike Turnesa 7 & 6

1949 Hermitage, Virginia
Sam Snead beat Johnny Palmer 3 & 2

1950 Scioto, Ohio
Chandler Harper beat Henry Williams Jnr 4 & 3

1951 Oakmont, Penns
Sam Snead beat Walter Burkemo 7 & 6

1952 Big Spring, Kentucky
Jim Turnesa beat Chick Harbert 1 hole

1953 Birmingham, Michigan
Walter Burkemo beat Felice Torza 2 & 1

1954 Keller, Minnesota
Chick Harbert beat Walter Burkemo 4 & 3

1955 Meadowbrook, Michigan
Doug Ford beat Cary Middlecoff 4 & 3

1956 Blue Hill, Mass
Jack Burke beat Ted Kroll 3 & 2

1957 Miami Valley, Ohio
Lionel Hebert beat Dow Finsterwald 2 & 1

1958 Llanerch, Penns
276 Dow Finsterwald 67-72-70-67
278 Billy Casper 73-67-68-70
280 Sam Snead 73-67-67-73

1959 Minneapolis, Minnesota
277 Bob Rosburg 71-72-68-66
278 Jerry Barber 69-65-71-73
Doug Sanders 72-66-68-72

1960 Firestone, Ohio
281 Jay Hebert 72-67-72-70
282 Jim Ferrier 71-74-66-71
283 Sam Snead 68-73-70-72
Doug Sanders 70-71-69-73

1961 Olympia Fields, Illinois
277 Jerry Barber 69-67-71-70
Don January 72-66-67-72
280 Doug Sanders 70-68-74-68
Barber won play-off, 67; January 68

1962 Aronimink, Penns
278 Gary Player (S Africa) 72-67-69-70
279 Bob Goalby 69-72-71-67
281 Jack Nicklaus 71-74-69-67
George Bayer 69-70-71-71

1963 Dallas, Texas
279 Jack Nicklaus 69-73-69-68
281 Dave Ragan 75-70-67-69
282 Dow Finsterwald 72-72-66-72
Bruce Crampton (Australia) 70-73-65-74

1964 Columbus, Ohio
271 Bobby Nichols 64-71-69-67
274 Arnold Palmer 68-68-69-69
Jack Nicklaus 67-73-70-64

1965 Laurel Valley, Penns
280 Dave Marr 70-69-70-71
282 Billy Casper 70-70-71-71
Jack Nicklaus 69-70-72-71

1966 Firestone, Ohio
280 Al Geiberger 68-72-68-72
284 Dudley Wysong 74-72-66-72

286 Billy Casper 73-73-70-70
Gene Littler 75-71-70-70
Gary Player
(S Africa) 73-70-70-73

1967 Columbine, Colorado
281 Don January 71-72-70-68
Don Massengale
70-75-70-66
282 Jack Nicklaus 67-75-69-71
Dan Sikes 69-70-70-73
January won play-off, 69; Massengale 71

1968 Pecan Valley, Texas
281 Julius Boros 71-71-70-69
282 Bob Charles (NZ)
72-70-70-70
Arnold Palmer
71-69-72-70

1969 Dayton, Ohio
276 Ray Floyd 69-66-67-74
277 Gary Player
(S Africa) 71-65-71-70
278 Bert Greene 71-68-68-71

1970 Southern Hills, Oklahoma
($200,000)
279 Dave Stockton
70-70-66-73 ($40,000)
281 Bob Murphy 71-73-71-66
Arnold Palmer
70-72-69-70

1971 PGA National, Florida
($200,000)
281 Jack Nicklaus
69-69-70-73 ($40,000)
283 Billy Casper 71-73-71-68
284 Tommy Bolt 72-74-69-69

1972 Oakland Hills, Michigan
($225,000)
281 Gary Player
(S Africa)
71-71-67-72 ($45,000)
283 Tommy Aaron
71-71-70-71
Jim Jamieson 69-72-72-70

1973 Canterbury, Ohio
($225,000)
277 Jack Nicklaus
72-68-68-69 ($45,000)
281 Bruce Crampton
(Australia) 71-73-67-70
282 Mason Rudolph
69-70-70-73
Lanny Wadkins
73-69-71-69
JC Snead 71-74-68-69

1974 Tanglewood, N Carolina
($225,000)
276 Lee Trevino
73-66-68-69 ($45,000)
277 Jack Nicklaus 69-69-70-69
279 Bobby Cole
(S Africa) 69-68-71-71
Hubert Green 68-68-73-70
Dave Hill 74-69-67-69
Sam Snead 69-71-71-68

1975 Firestone, Ohio
($225,000)
276 Jack Nicklaus
70-68-67-71 ($45,000)
278 Bruce Crampton
(Australia) 71-63-75-69
279 Tom Weiskopf
70-71-70-68

1976 Congressional, Maryland
($250,000)
281 Dave Stockton
70-72-69-70 ($45,000)
282 Raymond Floyd
72-68-71-71
Don January 70-69-71-72

1977 Pebble Beach, California
($250,000)
282 Lanny Wadkins
69-71-72-70 ($45,000)
Gene Littler 67-69-70-76
283 Jack Nicklaus 69-71-70-73
Wadkins won play-off at 3rd extra hole

1978 Oakmont, Penns
($300,000)
276 John Mahaffey
75-67-68-66 ($50,000)
Jerry Pate 72-70-66-68
Tom Watson 67-69-67-73
Mahaffey won play-off at 2nd extra hole

1979 Oakland Hills, Michigan
(350,000)
272 David Graham 69-68-70-65
(Australia ($60,000)

Ben Crenshaw
69-67-69-67
274 Randy Caldwell
67-70-66-71
Graham won play-off at 3rd extra hole
1980 Oak Hill, NY ($375,000)
274 Jack Nicklaus
70-69-66-69 ($60,000)
281 Andy Bean 72-71-68-70
283 Len Hinkle 70-69-69-75
Gil Morgan 68-70-73-72
1981 Atlanta, Georgia
($401,050)
273 Larry Nelson
70-66-66-71 ($60,000)
277 Fuzzy Zoeller 70-68-68-71
278 Dan Pohl 69-67-73-69
1982 Tulsa, Oklahoma
($450,000)
272 Raymond Floyd
63-69-68-72 ($65,000)
275 Lanny Wadkins
71-68-69-67
276 Fred Couples 67-71-72-66
Calvin Peete 69-70-68-69
1983 Riviera, California
($450,000)
274 Hal Sutton
65-66-72-71 ($65,000)
275 Jack Nicklaus 73-65-71-66
276 Peter Jacobsen
75-70-68-65

MAJOR OPEN CHAMPIONSHIPS

AUSTRALIAN OPEN CHAMPIONSHIP

Players Australian unless otherwise stated * amateur

1904 Kensington
324 Hon Michael Scott* (GB)
1905 Royal Melbourne
330 D Soutar
1906 Royal Sydney
322 Carnegie Clark
1907 Royal Melbourne
318 Hon Michael Scott* (GB)
1908 The Australian
311 Clyde Pearce*
1909 Royal Melbourne
316 Claude Felstead*
1910 Royal Adelaide
306 Carnegie Clark
1911 Royal Sydney
321 Carnegie Clark
1912 Royal Melbourne
321 Ivo Whitton*
1913 Royal Melbourne
302 Ivo Whitton*
1920 The Australian
290 Joe Kirkwood
1921 Royal Melbourne
295 A Le Fevre
1922 Royal Sydney
307 C Campbell
1923 Royal Adelaide
301 T Howard
1924 Royal Melbourne
303 A Russell*
1925 The Australian
299 F Popplewell
1926 Royal Adelaide
297 Ivo Whitton*
1927 Royal Melbourne
297 R Stewart
1928 Royal Sydney
295 F Popplewell
1929 Royal Adelaide
309 Ivo Whitton*
1930 Metropolitan
306 F Eyre
1931 The Australian
301 Ivo Whitton*

1932 Royal Adelaide
296 MJ Ryan*
1933 Royal Melbourne
302 ML Kelly
1934 Royal Sydney
283 WJ Bolger
1935 Royal Adelaide
293 F McMahon
1936 Metropolitan
282 Gene Sarazen (US)
1937 The Australian
299 G Naismith
1938 Royal Adelaide
283 Jim Ferrier*
1939 Royal Melbourne
285 Jim Ferrier*
1946 Royal Sydney
289 Ossie Pickworth
1947 Royal Queensland
285 Ossie Pickworth
1948 Kingston Heath
289 Ossie Pickworth
1949 The Australian
287 Eric Cremin
1950 Kooyonga
286 Norman von Nida
1951 Metropolitan
283 Peter Thomson
1952 Lake Karrinyup
278 Norman von Nida
1953 Royal Melbourne
278 Norman von Nida
1954 Kooyonga
280 Ossie Pickworth
1955 Gailes
290 Bobby Locke (S Africa)
1956 Royal Sydney
289 Bruce Crampton
1957 Kingston Heath
287 Frank Phillips
1958 Kooyonga
271 Gary Player (S Africa)
1959 The Australian
284 Kel Nagle
1960 Lake Karrinyup
282 Bruce Devlin*
1961 Victoria
275 Frank Phillips
1962 Royal Adelaide
281 Gary Player (S Africa)
1963 Royal Melbourne
278 Gary Player (S Africa)
1964 The Lakes
287 Jack Nicklaus (US)
1965 Kooyonga
264 Gary Player (S Africa)
1966 Royal Queensland
276 Arnold Palmer (US)
1967 Commonwealth
281 Peter Thomson
1968 Lake Karrinyup
270 Jack Nicklaus (US)
1969 Royal Sydney
288 Gary Player (S Africa)
1970 Kingston Heath
280 Gary Player (S Africa)
1971 Royal Hobart
269 Jack Nicklaus (US)
1972 Kooyonga
281 Peter Thomson
1973 Royal Queensland
280 JC Snead (US)
1974 Lake Karrinyup
279 Gary Player (S Africa)
1975 The Australian
279 Jack Nicklaus (US)
1976 The Australian
286 Jack Nicklaus (US)
1977 The Australian
284 David Graham
1978 The Australian
284 Jack Nicklaus (US)
1979 Metropolitan
288 Jack Newton
1980 The Lakes
284 Greg Norman
1981 Victoria
282 Bill Rogers (US)
1982 The Australian
287 Bob Shearer
1983 Kingston Heath
285 Peter Fowler

CANADIAN OPEN CHAMPIONSHIP

Players Canadian unless otherwise stated

1904 Montreal
156 JH Oke
1905 Toronto
146 George Cumming
1906 Ottawa
170 Charles Murray
1907 Toronto
300 Percy Barrett
1908 Montreal
300 Albert Murray
1909 Toronto
309 Karl Keffer
1910 Toronto
303 D Kenny
1911 Ottawa
314 Charles Murray
1912 Toronto
299 George Sargent
1913 Montreal
295 Albert Murray
1914 Toronto
300 Karl Keffer
1919 Hamilton
278 J Douglas Edgar (GB)
1920 Ottawa
298 J Douglas Edgar (GB)
1921 Toronto
293 William Trovinger
1922 Montreal
303 Al Watrous (US)
1923 Toronto
295 Clarence Hackney (US)
1924 Montreal
285 Leo Diegel (US)
1925 Toronto
295 Leo Diegel (US)
1926 Montreal
283 Macdonald Smith (US)
1927 Toronto
288 Tommy Armour (US)
1928 Toronto
282 Leo Diegel (US)
1929 Montreal
274 Leo Diegel (US)
1930 Hamilton
277 Tommy Armour (US)
1931 Toronto
292 Walter Hagen (US)
1932 Ottawa
290 Harry Cooper (US)
1933 Toronto
282 Joe Kirkwood (Australia)
1934 Toronto
287 Tommy Armour (US)
1935 Montreal
280 G Kunes
1936 Toronto
271 Lawson Little (US)
1937 Toronto
285 Harry Cooper (US)
1938 Toronto
277 Sam Snead (US)
1939 Saint John, New Brunswick
282 Jug McSpaden
1940 Toronto
281 Sam Snead (US)
1941 Toronto
274 Sam Snead (US)
1942 Toronto
275 Craig Wood (US)
1945 Toronto
280 Byron Nelson (US)
1946 Montreal
278 George Fazio (US)
1947 Toronto
268 Bobby Locke (S Africa)
1948 Vancouver
280 C Congdon (US)
1949 Toronto
271 Dutch Harrison (US)
1950 Montreal
271 Jim Ferrier (US)
1951 Toronto
273 Jim Ferrier (US)
1952 Winnipeg
263 Johnny Palmer (US)
1953 Toronto
273 Dave Douglas (US)
1954 Vancouver
280 Pat Fletcher
1955 Toronto
265 Arnold Palmer (US)
1956 Montreal
273 Doug Sanders* (US)
1957 Kitchener
271 George Bayer (US)

1958 Edmonton
267 Wes Ellis Jnr (US)
1959 Montreal
276 Doug Ford (US)
1960 Toronto
269 Art Wall (US)
1961 Winnipeg
270 Jack Cupit (US)
1962 Montreal
278 Ted Kroll (US)
1963 Toronto
280 Doug Ford (US)
1964 Montreal
277 Kel Nagle (Australia)
1965 Toronto
273 Gene Littler (US)
1966 Vancouver
280 Don Massengale (US)
1967 Montreal
279 Billy Casper (US)
1968 Toronto
274 Bob Charles (NZ)
1969 Montreal
275 Tommy Aaron (US)
1970 London, Ontario
279 Kermit Zarley (US)
1971 Montreal
275 Lee Trevino (US)
1972 Ridgeway, Ontario
275 Gay Brewer (US)
1973 Quebec
278 Tom Weiskopf (US)
1974 Mississauga, Toronto
270 Bobby Nichols (US)
1975 Royal Montreal
274 Tom Weiskopf (US)
1976 Essex Windsor
267 Jerry Pate (US)
1977 Glen Abbey, Oakville, Ontario
280 Lee Trevino (US)
1978 Glen Abbey, Oakville, Ontario
283 Bruce Lietzke (US)
1979 Glen Abbey, Oakville, Ontario
281 Lee Trevino (US)
1980 Royal Montreal
274 Bob Gilder (US)
1981 Glen Abbey, Oakville, Ontario
280 Peter Oosterhuis (GB)
1982 Glen Abbey, Oakville, Ontario
277 Bruce Lietzke (US)
1983 Glen Abbey, Oakville, Ontario
277 John Cook (US)

JAPANESE OPEN CHAMPIONSHIP

Players from Japan, unless otherwise stated

1927 Hodogaya
309 R Akahoshi*
1928 Tokio
301 R Asami
1929 Ibaraki
298 T Miyamoto
1930 Ibaraki
287 T Miyamoto
1931 Hodogaya
281 R Asami
1932 Ibaraki
298 T Miyamoto
1933 Kasumigaseki
294 K Nakamura
1934 cancelled due to typhoon
1935 Asaka
293 T Miyamoto
1936 Inagawa
296 T Miyamoto
1937 Sagami
284 Chin Sei Sui
1938 Fujisawa
294 RM Fuku
1939 Hirono
287 T Toda
1940 Asaka
285 T Miyamoto
1941 Hodogaya
290 En Toku Shun (Korea)
1950 Abiko
288 Y Hayashi
1951 Inagawa
284 Son Shi Kin
1952 Kawana
278 T Nakamura
1953 Takarazuka
299 Son Shi Kin
1954 Tokio
291 Y Hayashi
1955 Hirono
293 K Ono

1956 Kasumigaseki
281 T Nakamura
1957 Aichi
285 H Kobari
1958 Takanodai
288 T Nakamura
1959 Sagamihara
298 Chen Ching-Po
1960 Hirono
296 H Kobari
1961 Takanodai
289 K Hosoishi
1962 Chiba
287 T Sugihara
1963 Yokkaichi
283 T Toda
1964 Tokio
288 H Sugimoto
1965 Miyoshi
284 T Kitta
1966 Sodegaura
285 S Sato
1967 Hirono
282 T Kitta
1968 Sobu
284 T Kono
1969 Ono
284 H Sugimoto
1970 Musashi
282 M Kitta
1971 Aichi
282 Y Fujii
1972 Iwai City
278 H Chang Sang (S Korea)
1973 Osaka
278 B Arda (Philippines)
1974 Central
279 M Ozaki
1975 Kasugai
278 T Murakami
1976 Central
288 K Shimada
1977 Narashino
284 S Ballesteros (Spain)
1978 Yokohama
281 S Ballesteros (Spain)
1979 Hino, Kyoto
285 Kuo Chie-Hsiung (Taiwan)
1980 Sagamihara
296 K Kikuchi
1981 Nihon Rhine
280 Y Hagawa
1982 Musashi Toyooka
277 A Yabe
1983 Rokko-Kokusai
281 I Aoki (after tie with T Gale)

SOUTH AFRICAN OPEN CHAMPIONSHIP

Players from South Africa, unless otherwise stated

1907 Kimberley
147 Lawrence Waters
1908 Johannesburg
163 George Fotheringham
1909 Potchefstroom
306 John Fotheringham
1910 Wynberg
315 George Fotheringham
1911 Durban
301 George Fotheringham
1912 Potchefstroom
305 George Fotheringham
1913 Kimberley
304 JAW Prentice*
1914 Wynberg
299 George Fotheringham
1919 Durban
320 WH Horne
1920 Johannesburg
302 LB Waters
1921 Port Elizabeth
316 Jack Brews (GB)
1922 Port Alfred
310 F Jangle
1923 Royal Cape
305 Jack Brews (GB)
1924 Durban
316 BH Elkin
1925 Johannesburg
295 Sid Brews (GB)
1926 Port Elizabeth
301 Jack Brews (GB)
1927 Maccauvlei
301 Sid Brews (GB)
1928 Durban
297 Jack Brews (GB)
1929 Royal Cape
315 A Tosh
1930 East London
297 Sid Brews (GB)

1931 Port Elizabeth
302 Sid Brews (GB)
1932 Mowbray
304 C McIlvenny
1933 Maccauvlei
297 Sid Brews (GB)
1934 Port Elizabeth
319 Sid Brews (GB)
1935 Johannesburg
296 Bobby Locke*
1936 Royal Cape
297 CE Olander*
1937 East London
288 Bobby Locke*
1938 Maccauvlei
279 Bobby Locke
1939 Royal Durban
279 Bobby Locke
1940 Port Elizabeth
293 Bobby Locke
1946 Royal Johannesburg
285 Bobby Locke
1947 Mowbray, Cape Town
293 RW Glennie*
1948 East London
298 M Janks*
1949 Maccauvlei
291 Sid Brews (GB)
1950 Durban
289 Bobby Locke
1951 Houghton
275 Bobby Locke
1952 Humewood
300 Sid Brews (GB)
1953 Royal Cape
302 JR Boyd*
1954 East London
289 Reg Taylor*
1955 Zwartkop
283 Bobby Locke
1956 Durban
286 Gary Player
1957 Humewood
289 Harold Henning
1958 Bloemfontein
281 AA Stewart*
1959 Johannesburg
282 Denis Hutchinson*
1960 Mowbray
288 Gary Player
1961 East London
289 Retief Waltman
1962 Johannesburg
285 Harold Henning
1963 Durban
281 Retief Waltman
1964 Bloemfontein
278 Alan Henning
1965 Cape Town
273 Gary Player
1966 Johannesburg
274 Gary Player
1967 East London
279 Gary Player
1968 Houghton
278 Gary Player
1969 Durban
273 Gary Player
1970 Royal Durban
285 Tommy Horton (GB)
1971 Mowbray, Cape Town
276 Simon Hobday (Rhodesia)
1972 Royal Johannesburg
274 Gary Player
1973 Durban
282 Bob Charles (NZ)
1974 Royal Johannesburg
272 Bobby Cole
1975 Mowbray, Cape Town
278 Gary Player
1976 Houghton
287 Dale Hayes
1976 Durban
280 Gary Player
1977 Royal Johannesburg
273 Gary Player
1978 Mowbray
285 Hugh Baiocchi
1979 Houghton
279 Gary Player
1980 Durban
279 Bobby Cole
1981 Royal Johannesburg
272 Gary Player
1982 Cape Town
278 Charlie Bolling (US)
1983 Royal Cape
278 Charles Bolling

THE AMATEURS

AMATEUR CHAMPIONSHIP

Players British, unless otherwise stated

1885 Hoylake
AF MacFie beat HG Hutchinson 7 & 6
1886 St Andrews
HG Hutchinson beat HA Lamb 7 & 6
1887 Hoylake
HG Hutchinson beat J Ball 1 hole
1888 Prestwick
J Ball beat JE Laidlay 5 & 4
1889 St Andrews
JE Laidlay beat LMB Melville 2 & 1
1890 Hoylake
J Ball Jnr beat JE Laidlay 4 & 3
1891 St Andrews
LE Laidlay beat HH Hilton at 20th
1892 Royal St George's
J Ball beat HH Hilton 3 & 1
1893 Prestwick
PC Anderson beat JE Laidlay 1 hole
1894 Hoylake
J Ball beat SM Fergusson 1 hole
1895 St Andrews
LMB Melville beat J Ball at 19th
1896 Royal St George's
FG Tait beat HH Hilton 8 & 7
1897 Muirfield
AJT Allan beat J Robb 4 & 2
(36-hole final from this year)
1898 Hoylake
FG Tait beat SM Fergusson 7 & 5
1899 Prestwick
J Ball beat FG Tait at 37th
1900 Royal St George's, Sandwich
HH Hilton beat J Robb 8 & 7
1901 St Andrews
HH Hilton beat JL Low 1 hole
1902 Hoylake
C Hutchings beat SH Fry 1 hole
1903 Muirfield
R Maxwell beat HG Hutchinson 7 & 5
1904 Royal St George's, Sandwich
WJ Travis (US) beat E Blackwell 4 & 3
1905 Prestwick
AG Barry beat Hon O Scott 3 & 2
1906 Hoylake
J Robb beat CC Lingen 4 & 3
1907 St Andrews
J Ball Jnr beat CA Palmer 6 & 4
1908 Royal St George's
EA Lassen beat HE Taylor 7 & 6
1909 Muirfield
R Maxwell beat CK Hutchison 1 hole
1910 Hoylake
J Ball beat CC Aylmer 10 & 9
1911 Prestwick
HH Hilton beat EA Lassen 4 & 3
1912 Westward Ho!
J Ball beat A Mitchell at 38th
1913 St Andrews
HH Hilton beat R Harris 6 & 5
1914 Royal St George's, Sandwich
JLC Jenkins beat CO Hezlet 3 & 2
1915-1918 No championship
1920 Muirfield
CJH Tolley beat RA Gardner (US) at 37th
1921 Hoylake
WI Hunter beat AJ Graham 12 & 11
1922 Prestwick
EWE Holderness beat J Caven 1 hole
1923 Deal
RH Wethered beat R Harris 7 & 6

1924 St Andrews
EWE Holderness beat EF Storey 3 & 2
1925 Westward Ho!
R Harris beat KF Fradgley 13 & 12
1926 Muirfield
J Sweetser (US) beat AF Simpson 6 & 5
1927 Hoylake
Dr W Tweddell beat DE Landale 7 & 6
1928 Prestwick
TP Perkins beat RH Wethered 6 & 4
1929 Royal St George's, Sandwich
CJH Tolley beat JN Smith 4 & 3
1930 St Andrews
RT Jones Jnr (US) beat RH Wethered 7 & 6
1931 Westward Ho!
E Martin Smith beat J de Forest 1 hole
1932 Muirfield
J de Forest beat EW Fiddian 3 & 1
1933 Hoylake
Hon M Scott beat TA Bourn 4 & 3
1934 Prestwick
W Lawson Little (US) beat J Wallace 14 & 13
1935 Royal Lytham
W Lawson Little (US) beat W Tweddell 1 hole
1936 St Andrews
H Thomson beat J Ferrier (Australia) 2 holes
1937 Royal St George's, Sandwich
R Sweeney (US) beat LOM Munn 3 & 2
1938 Troon
CR Yates (US) beat C Ewing 3 & 2
1939 Hoylake
AT Kyle beat AA Duncan 2 & 1
1940-1945 No championship
1946 Royal Birkdale
J Bruen beat R Sweeney (US) 4 & 3
1947 Carnoustie
WP Turnesa (US) beat RD Chapman (US) 3 & 2
1948 Royal St George's, Sandwich
FR Stranahan (US) beat C Stowe 5 & 4
1949 Portmarnock
SM McCready beat WP Turnesa (US) 2 & 1
1950 St Andrews
FR Stranahan (US) beat RD Chapman (US) 8 & 6
1951 Porthcawl
RD Chapman (US) beat CR Coe (US) 5 & 4
1952 Prestwick
EH Ward (US) beat FR Stranahan (US) 7 & 5
1953 Hoylake
JB Carr beat EH Ward (US) 2 holes
1954 Muirfield
DW Bachli (Australia) beat WC Campbell (US) 2 & 1
1955 Royal Lytham
JW Conrad (US) beat A Slater 3 & 2
1956 Troon
JC Beharrell beat LG Taylor 5 & 4
1957 Formby
R Reid Jack beat HB Ridgley (US) 2 & 1
1958 St Andrews
JB Carr beat A Thirlwell 3 & 2
1959 Sandwich
DR Beman (US) beat W Hyndman III (US) 3 & 2
1960 Portrush
JB Carr beat R Cochran (US) 8 & 7
1961 Turnberry
MF Bonallack beat J Walker 6 & 4
1962 Hoylake
RD Davies (US) beat J Povall 1 hole
1963 St Andrews
MSR Lunt beat JG Blackwell 2 & 1

1964 Ganton
GJ Clark beat MSR Lunt at 39th
1965 Porthcawl
MF Bonallack beat CA Clark 2 & 1
1966 Carnoustie
RE Cole (S Africa) beat RDBM Shade 3 & 2
1967 Formby
RB Dickson (US) beat RJ Cerrudo (US) 2 & 1
1968 Troon
MF Bonallack beat JB Carr 7 & 6
1969 Hoylake
MF Bonallack beat W Hyndman (US) 3 & 2
1970 Newcastle, County Down
MF Bonallack beat W Hyndman (US) 8 & 7
1971 Carnoustie
S Melnyk (US) beat J Simons (US) 3 & 2
1972 Royal St George's, Sandwich
T Homer beat A Thirlwell 4 & 3
1973 Royal Porthcawl
R Siderowf (US) beat P Moody 5 & 3
1974 Muirfield
T Homer beat J Gabrielsen 2 holes
1975 Royal Liverpool, Hoylake
M Giles III (US) beat M James 8 & 7
1976 St Andrews
R Siderowf (US) beat JC Davies at 37th
1977 Ganton
PM McEvoy beat HM Campbell 5 & 4
1978 Royal Troon
PM McEvoy beat P McKellar 4 & 3
1979 Hillside
J Sigel (US) beat S Hoch (US) 3 & 2
1980 Royal Porthcawl
D Evans beat DR Suddards (S Africa) 4 & 3
1981 St Andrews
P Ploujoux (France) beat J Hirsch (US) 4 & 2
1982 Deal
MS Thompson beat AK Stubbs 4 & 3
1983
P Parkin beat J Holtgrieve (US) 5 & 4

AMERICAN AMATEUR CHAMPIONSHIP

1893 Newport, Rhode Island
WG Lawrence bt CB Macdonald 4 & 3
1894 St Andrews
LB Stoddart bt CB Macdonald 5 & 4
1895 Newport, Rhode Island
CB Macdonald bt CE Sands 12 & 11
1896 Shinnecock Hills, NY
HJ Whigham bt JG Thorp 8 & 7
1897 Chicago, Illinois
HJ Whigham bt WR Betts 8 & 6
1898 Morris County, New Jersey
FS Douglas bt WB Smith 5 & 3
1899 Onwentsia, Illinois
HM Harriman bt FS Douglas 3 & 2
1900 Garden City, NY
WJ Travis (Australia) bt FS Douglas 2 holes
1901 Atlantic City, New Jersey
WJ Travis (Australia) bt WE Egan 5 & 4
1902 Glen View, Illinois
LN James bt EM Byers 4 & 2
1903 Nassau, NY
WJ Travis (Australia) bt EM Byers 5 & 4
1904 Baltusrol, New Jersey
HC Egan bt F Herreshoff 8 & 6

1905 Chicago, Illinois
HC Egan bt DE Sawyer 6 & 5
1906 Englewood, New Jersey
EM Byers bt GS Lyon 2 holes
1907 Euclid, Ohio
JD Travers bt A Graham 6 & 5
1908 Garden City, NY
JD Travers bt M Behr 8 & 7
1909 Chicago, Illinois
RA Gardner bt HC Egan 4 & 3
1910 The Country Club, Brookline
WC Fownes Jnr bt WK Wood 4 & 3
1911 Apawamis, NY
HH Hilton (GB) bt F Herreshoff at 37th
1912 Chicago, Illinois
JD Travers bt C Evans 7 & 6
1913 Garden City, NY
JD Travers bt JG Anderson 5 & 4
1914 Ekwanok, Vermont
FD Ouimet bt JD Travers 6 & 5
1915 Detroit, Michigan
RA Gardner bt JG Anderson 5 & 4
1916 Merion, Penns
C Evans bt RA Gardner 4 & 3
1919 Oakmont, Penns
SD Herron bt RT Jones Jnr 5 & 4
1920 Engineers, NY
C Evans bt F Ouimet 7 & 6
1921 St Louis, Missouri
JP Guilford bt RA Gardner 7 & 6
1922 The Country Club, Brookline
JW Sweetser bt C Evans 3 & 2
1923 Flossmoor, Illinois
MR Marston bt JW Sweetser at 38th
1924 Merion, Penns
RT Jones Jnr bt G von Elm 9 & 8
1925 Oakmont, Penns
RT Jones Jnr bt W Gunn 8 & 7
1926 Baltusrol, New Jersey
G von Elm bt RT Jones Jnr 2 & 1
1927 Minikahda Club, Minnesota
RT Jones Jnr bt C Evans Jnr 8 & 7
1928 Brae Burn, Mass
RT Jones Jnr bt TP Perkins 10 & 9
1929 Del Monte, California
HR Johnston bt OF Willing 4 & 3
1930 Merion, Penns
RT Jones Jnr bt EV Homans 8 & 7
1931 Beverly, Illinois
F Ouimet bt J Westland 6 & 5
1932 Baltimore, Maryland
C Ross Sommerville (Canada) bt J Goodman 2 & 1
1933 Kenwood, Ohio
GT Dunlap bt MR Marston 6 & 5
1934 The Country Club, Brookline
W Lawson Little bt D Goldman 8 & 7
1935 Cleveland, Ohio
W Lawson Little bt W Emery 4 & 2
1936 Garden City, NY
JW Fischer bt J McLean (GB) at 37th
1937 Alderwood, Oregon
JW Goodman bt R Billows 2 holes
1938 Oakmont, Penns
WP Turnesa bt BP Abbott 8 & 7
1939 North Shore, Illinois
M Ward bt R Billows 7 & 5
1940 Winged Foot, NY
RD Chapman bt W McCullogh 11 & 9
1941 Omaha Field, Nebraska
M Ward bt BP Abbott 4 & 3
1946 Baltusrol, New Jersey
SE Bishop bt SL Quick at 37th
1947 Pebble Beach, California
RH Riegel bt JW Dawson 2 & 1
1948 Memphis, Tennessee
WP Turnesa bt RE Billows 2 & 1
1949 Oak Hill, NY
CR Coe bt R King 11 & 10
1950 Minneapolis, Minnesota
S Urzetta bt FR Stranahan at 39th
1951 Saucon Valley, Penns
B Maxwell bt JF Gagliardi 4 & 3
1952 Seattle, Washington
J Westland bt A Mengert 3 & 2

1953 Oklahoma City
G Littler bt D Morey 1 hole
1954 Detroit, Michigan
AD Palmer bt R Sweeney 1 hole
1955 Virginia CC
EH Ward bt W Hyndman 9 & 8
1956 Knollwood Club, Illinois
EH Ward bt C Kocsis 5 & 4
1957 The Country Club, Brookline
H Robbins bt FM Taylor 5 & 4
1958 Olympic, California
CR Coe bt TD Aaron 5 & 4
1959 Broadmoor, Colorado
JW Nicklaus bt CR Coe 1 hole
1960 St Louis, Minnesota
DR Beman bt RW Gardner 6 & 4
1961 Pebble Beach, California
JW Nicklaus bt HD Wysong 8 & 6
1962 Pinehurst, N Carolina
LE Harris Jnr bt D Gray 1 hole
1963 Wakonda, Iowa
DR Beman bt RH Sikes 2 & 1
1964 Canterbury, Ohio
WC Campbell bt E Tutwiler 1 hole
(Stroke play introduced)
1965 Southern Hills, Oklahoma
291 RJ Murphy Jnr 73-69-76-73
292 RB Dickson 71-75-72-74
1966 Merion, Penns
285 G Cowan (Canada) 74-72-72-67
285 DR Beman 71-67 76-71
Cowan won play-off, 75; Beman 76
1967 Broadmoor, Colorado
285 RB Dickson 71-71-74-69
286 MM Giles III 76-69-72-69
1968 Scioto, Ohio
286 B Fleisher 73-70-71-70
285 MM Giles III 75-72-73-65
1969 Oakmont, Penns
286 SN Melnyk 70-73-73-70
291 MM Giles III 72-75-72-72
1970 Waverley, Oregon
279 L Wadkins 67-73-69-70
280 T Kite 69-67-62-73
1971 Wilmington, Delaware
280 G Cowan (Canada) 70-71-69-70
283 E Pearce 70-69-73-71
1972 Charlotte, N Carolina
285 MM Giles III 73-68-72-72
288 MS Hayes 73-72-69-74
B Crenshaw 71-75-71-71
(Reverted to matchplay)
1973 Inverness, Illinois
C Stadler bt D Strawn 6 & 5
1974 Ridgewood, New Jersey
J Pate bt JP Grace 2 & 1
1975 Virginia CC, Richmond
FS Ridley bt K Fergus 2 holes
1976 Bel-Air, Los Angeles
B Sander bt C Parker Moore Jnr 8 & 6
1977 Aronimink, Penns
J Fought bt DH Fischesser 9 & 8
1978 Plainfield, New Jersey
J Cook bt S Hoch 5 & 4
1979 Canterbury, Cleveland, Ohio
M O'Meara bt J Cook 8 & 7
1980 The Country Club, N Carolina
H Sutton bt B Lewis 9 & 8
1981 Olympic Club, California
N Crosby bt B Lindley at 37th
1982 The Country Club, Brookline
J Sigel bt D Tolley 8 & 7
1983 North Shore, Glenview, Illinois
J Sigel bt C Perry 8 & 7

THE WOMEN'S CHAMPIONSHIPS

BRITISH WOMEN'S AMATEUR

1893 St Annes
Lady Margaret Scott
1894 Littlestone
Lady Margaret Scott
1895 Portrush
Lady Margaret Scott
1896 Hoylake
Amy Pascoe
1897 Gullane
Edith Orr
1898 Yarmouth
L Thomson
1899 Newcastle, Co Down
May Hezlet
1900 Westward Ho!
Rhona Adair
1901 Aberdovey
Molly Graham
1902 Deal
May Hezlet
1903 Portrush
Rhona Adair
1904 Troon
Lottie Dod
1905 Cromer
B Thompson
1906 Burnham
Mrs Kennion
1907 Newcastle, Co Down
May Hezlet
1908 St Andrews
M Titterton
1909 Birkdale
Dorothy Campbell
1910 Westward Ho!
Miss Grant Suttie
1911 Portrush
Dorothy Campbell
1912 Turnberry
Gladys Ravenscroft
1913 St Annes
Muriel Dodd
1914 Hunstanton
Cecil Leitch
1915-18 no championship
1919
Cancelled owing to rail strike
1920 Newcastle, Co Down
Cecil Leitch
1921 Turnberry
Cecil Leitch
1922 Prince's, Sandwich
Joyce Wethered
1923 Burnham
Doris Chambers
1924 Portrush
Joyce Wethered
1925 Troon
Joyce Wethered
1926 Harlech
Cecil Leitch
1927 Newcastle, Co Down
Miss T de la Chaume (France)
1928 Hunstanton
Nanette Le Blan (France)
1929 St Andrews
Joyce Wethered
1930 Formby
Diana Fishwick
1931 Portmarnock
Enid Wilson
1932 Saunton
Enid Wilson
1933 Gleneagles
Enid Wilson
1934 Royal Porthcawl
Helen Holm
1935 Newcastle, Co Down
Wanda Morgan
1936 Southport and Ainsdale
Pam Barton
1937 Turnberry
Jessie Anderson
1938 Burnham
Helen Holm
1939 Portrush
Pam Barton
1940-45 no championship

1946 Hunstanton
Jean Hetherington
1947 Gullane
Babe Zaharias (US)
1948 Royal Lytham
Louise Suggs (US)
1949 Harlech
Frances Stephens
1950 Newcastle, Co Down
Vicomtesse de St Sauveur (France)
1951 Broadstone
PG MacCann
1952 Troon
Moira Paterson
1953 Porthcawl
Marlene Stewart
1954 Ganton
Frances Stephens
1955 Portrush
Jessie Valentine
1956 Sunningdale
Margaret Smith
1957 Gleneagles
Philomena Garvey
1958 Hunstanton
Jessie Valentine
1959 Ascot
Elizabeth Price
1960 Harlech
Barbara McIntire (US)
1961 Carnoustie
Marley Spearman
1962 Royal Birkdale
Marley Spearman
1963 Newcastle, Co Down
Brigitte Varangot (France)
1964 Prince's Sandwich
Carol Sorenson (US)
1965 St Andrews
Brigitte Varangot (France)
1966 Ganton
Elizabeth Chadwick
1967 Harlech
Elizabeth Chadwick
1968 Walton Heath
Brigitte Varangot (France)
1969 Portrush
Catherine Lacoste (France)
1970 Gullane
Dinah Oxley
1971 Alwoodley
Michelle Walker
1972 Hunstanton
Michelle Walker
1973 Carnoustie
Ann Irvin
1974 Royal Porthcawl
Carol Semple (US)
1975 St Andrews
Nancy Syms (US)
1976 Silloth
Cathy Panton
1977 Hillside
Angela Uzielli
1978 Notts
Edwina Kennedy (Australia)
1979 Nairn
Maureen Madill
1980 Woodhall Spa
Anne Sander (US)
1981 Caernarvonshire
Belle Robertson
1982 Walton Heath
Kitrina Douglas
1983 Silloth
Jill Thornhill

US WOMEN'S OPEN

1946 Spokane, Washington
Patty Berg
1947 Starmount Forest CC
Betty Jameson
1948 Atlantic City CC
Mildred Zaharias
1949 Prince Georges G&CC
Louise Suggs
1950 Rolling Hills CC
Mildred Zaharias
1951 Druid Hills GC
Betsy Rawls

1952 Bala GC
Louise Suggs
Taken over by USGA
1953 CC of Rochester
Betsy Rawls
1954 Salem CC
Mildred Zaharias
1955 Wichita CC
Fay Crocker
1956 Northland CC
Kathy Cornelius
1957 Winged Foot
Betsy Rawls
1958 Forest Lake CC
Mickey Wright
1959 Churchill Valley CC
Mickey Wright
1960 Worcester CC
Betsy Rawls
1961 Baltusrol GC (lower)
Mickey Wright
1962 Dunes Golf & Beach Club
Murle Lindstrom
1963 Kenwood CC
Mary Mills
1964 San Diego CC
Mickey Wright
1965 Atlantic City CC
Carol Mann
1966 Hazeltine National GC
Sandra Spuzich
1967 Hot Springs, Virginia
Catherine Lacoste
1968 Moselem Springs GC
Susie Berning
1969 Scenic Hills CC
Donna Caponi
1970 Muskogee CC
Donna Caponi
1971 Kahkwa Club
JoAnne Carner
1972 Winged Foot
Susie Berning
1973 CC of Rochester
Susie Berning
1974 La Grange CC
Sandra Haynie
1975 Atlantic City CC
Sandra Palmer
1976 Rolling Green GC
JoAnne Carner
1977 Hazeltine National
Hollis Stacy
1978 Indianapolis CC
Hollis Stacy
1979 Brooklawn CC
Jerilyn Britz
1980 Richland CC
Amy Alcott
1981 La Grange CC
Pat Bradley
1982 Broadmoor
Julie Inkster
1983 Canoe Brook CC
Joanne Pacillo

THE TEAM CHAMPIONSHIPS

RYDER CUP

1927 Worcester, Mass
US 9½, Great Britain 2½
1929 Moortown, Leeds
Great Britain 7, US 5
1931 Scioto, Ohio
US 9, Great Britain 3
1933 Southport & Ainsdale, Lancs
Great Britain 6½, US 5½
1935 Ridgewood, New Jersey
US 9, Great Britain 3
1937 Southport & Ainsdale, Lancs
US 8, Great Britain 4
1947 Portland, Oregon
US 11, Great Britain 1
1949 Ganton, Yorkshire
US 7, Great Britain 5

1951 Pinehurst, N Carolina
US 9½, Great Britain 2½
1953 Wentworth, Surrey
US 6½, Great Britain 5½
1955 Palm Springs, California
US 8, Great Britain 4
1957 Lindrick, Sheffield
Great Britain 7½, US 4½
1959 Palm Desert, California
US 8½, Great Britain 3½
1961 Royal Lytham, Lancs
US 14½, Great Britain 9½
1963 Atlanta, Georgia
US 23, Great Britain 9
1965 Royal Birkdale, Lancs
US 19½, Great Britain 12½
1967 Houston Texas
US 23½, Great Britain 8½
1969 Royal Birkdale, Lancs
US 16, Great Britain 16
1971 St Louis, Missouri
US 18½, Great Britain 13½
1973 Muirfield, E Lothian
US 19, GB & Ireland 13
1975 Laurel Valley, Penns
US 21, GB & Ireland 11
1977 Royal Lytham, Lancs
US 12½, GB & Ireland 7½
1979 Greenbrier, W Virginia
US 17, Europe 11
1981 Walton Heath, Surrey
US 18½, Europe 9½
1983 PGA National, Florida
US 14½, Europe 13½

WALKER CUP

1922 National Links, Long Island, NY
US 8, GB & Ireland 4
1923 St Andrews, Scotland
US 6½, GB & Ireland 5½
1924 Garden City, NY
US 9, GB & Ireland 3
1926 St Andrews, Scotland
US 6½, GB & Ireland 5½
1928 Chicago GC, Illinois
US 11, GB & Ireland 1
1930 Royal St George's, Sandwich
US 10, GB & Ireland 2
1932 Country Club Brooklyn, Mass
US 9½, GB & Ireland 2½
1934 St Andrews, Scotland
US 9½, GB & Ireland 2½
1936 Pine Valley, New Jersey
US 10½, GB & Ireland 1½
1938 St Andrews, Scotland
GB & Ireland 7½, US 4½
1947 St Andrews, Scotland
US 8, GB & Ireland 4
1949 Winged Foot, NY
US 10, GB & Ireland 2
1951 Royal Birkdale, Lancs
US 7½, GB & Ireland 4½
1953 Merion, Mass
US 9, GB & Ireland 3
1955 St Andrews, Scotland
US 10, GB & Ireland 2
1957 Minikahdu, Minnesota
US 8½, GB & Ireland 3½
1959 Muirfield, Scotland
US 9, GB & Ireland 3
1961 Seattle, Washington
US 11, GB & Ireland 1
1963 Turnberry, Scotland
US 14, GB & Ireland 10
1965 Baltimore, Maryland
US 12, GB & Ireland 12
1967 Royal St George's Sandwich
US 15, GB & Ireland 9
1969 Milwaukee, Wisconsin
US 13, GB & Ireland 11
1971 St Andrews, Scotland
GB & Ireland 13, US 11
1973 Brooklyn, Mass
US 14, GB & Ireland 10
1975 St Andrews, Scotland
US 15½, GB & Ireland 8½
1977 Shinnecock Hills, NY
US 16, GB & Ireland 8
1979 Muirfield, Scotland
US 15½, GB & Ireland 8½
1981 Cypress Point, California
US 15, GB & Ireland 9
1982 Royal Liverpool, England
US 13½, GB & Ireland 10½

CURTIS CUP

1932 Wentworth, Surrey
US 5½, GB & Ireland 3½
1934 Chevy Chase, Maryland
US 6½, GB & Ireland 2½
1936 Gleneagles, Scotland
US 4½, GB & Ireland 4½
1938 Essex CC, Mass
US 5½, GB & Ireland 3½
1948 Royal Birkdale, Lancs
US 6½, GB & Ireland 2½
1950 Buffalo, NY
US 7½, GB & Ireland 1½
1952 Muirfield, Scotland
GB & Ireland 5, US 4
1954 Merion, Penns
US 6, GB & Ireland 3
1956 Prince's, England
GB & Ireland 5, US 4
1958 Brae Burn, Mass
GB & Ireland 4½, US 4½
1960 Lindrick, Yorkshire
US 6½, GB & Ireland 2½
1962 Broadmoor, Colorado Springs
US 8, GB & Ireland 1
1964 Royal Porthcawl, Wales
US 10½, GB & Ireland 7½
1966 Cascades, Hot Springs, Virginia
US 13, GB & Ireland 5
1968 Royal County Down, Ireland
US 10½, GB & Ireland 7½
1970 Brae Burn, Mass
US 11½, GB & Ireland 6½
1972 Western Gailes, Scotland
US 10, GB & Ireland 8
1974 San Francisco, California
US 13, GB & Ireland 5
1976 Royal Lytham, Lancs
US 11½, GB & Ireland 6½
1978 Apawamis, NY
US 12, GB & Ireland 6
1980 St Pierre, Chepstow, Wales
US 13, GB & Ireland 5
1982 Denver, Colorado
US 14½, GB & Ireland 3½

WORLD CUP

1953 Beaconsfield, Montreal
287 Argentina
Roberto de Vicenzo 147
Tony Cerda 140
1954 Laval Sur Le Lac, Montreal
556 Australia
Peter Thomson 277
Kel Nagle 279
1955 Columbia, Washington
560 US
Chick Harbert 281
Ed Furgol 279
1956 Wentworth, Surrey
567 US
Ben Hogan 277
Sam Snead 290
1957 Kasumigaseki, Tokyo
557 Japan
Torakichi Nakamura 274
Koichi Ono 283
1958 Club de Golf, Mexico City
579 Ireland
Harry Bradshaw 286
Christy O'Connor 293
1959 Royal Melbourne
563 Australia
Peter Thomson 275
Kel Nagle 288
1960 Portmarnock, Dublin
565 US
Arnold Palmer 284
Sam Snead 281
1961 Dorado Beach, Puerto Rico
560 US
Sam Snead 272
Jimmy Demaret 288
1962 Jockey Club, Buenos Aires
557 US
Arnold Palmer 278
Sam Snead 279
1963 St Nom La Breteche, Paris
482 US
Jack Nicklaus 237
Arnold Palmer 245

1964 Royal Kaanapali, Maui
554 US
Arnold Palmer 278
Jack Nicklaus 276

1965 Club de Campo, Madrid
571 South Africa
Gary Player 281
Harold Henning 290

1966 Yomiuri, Tokyo
548 US
Jack Nicklaus 273
Arnold Palmer 275

1967 Club de Golf, Mexico City
557 US
Arnold Palmer 276
Jack Nicklaus 281

1968 Olgiata, Rome
569 Canada
Al Balding 274
George Knudson 295

1969 Singapore Island
552 US
Lee Trevino 275
Orville Moody 277

1970 Jockey Club, Buenos Aires
544 Australia
David Graham 270
Bruce Devlin 274

1971 PGA National, Palm Beach
555 US
Jack Nicklaus 271
Lee Trevino 284

1972 Royal Melbourne
438 Taiwan
Hsieh Min Nam 217
Lu Liang Huan 221

1973 Golf Nueva Andalucia, Marbella
558 US
Johnny Miller 277
Jack Nicklaus 281

1974 Lagunita, Venezuela
554 South Africa
Bobby Cole 271
Dale Hayes 283

1975 Navatanee, Bangkok
554 US
Lou Graham 279
Johnny Miller 275

1976 Mission Hills, Palm Springs
574 Spain
Manuel Pinero 285
Severiano Ballesteros 289

1977 Wack Wack, Manila
591 Spain
Severiano Ballesteros 295
Antonio Garrido 296

1978 Princeville Maka, Hawai
564 US
John Mahaffey 281
Andy North 283

1979 Glyfada, Athens
575 US
John Mahaffey 290
Hale Irwin 285

1980 El Rignon, Bogota
572 Canada
Dan Halldorson 285
Jim Nelford 287

1981 no competition

1982 Acapulco, Mexico
563 Spain
Manuel Pinero 281
José Canizares 282

1983 Pondok Indah, Indonesia
565 United States
Rex Caldwell 279
John Cook 286

MEN'S WORLD AMATEUR TEAM CHAMPIONSHIP (EISENHOWER TROPHY)

1958 St Andrews, Scotland
918 Australia (B Devlin, P Toogood, R Stevens, D Bachli)

1960 Merion, US
834 United States (D Beman, R Gardner, W Hyndman, J Nicklaus)

1962 Fuji GC, Japan
854 United States (D Beman, WJ Patton, R Sikes, L Harris)

1964 Olgiata, Italy
895 Great Britain (R Shade, R Foster, M Lunt, M Bonallack)
1966 Mexico City
877 Australia (K Hartley, P Billings, W Berwick, K Donohoe)
1968 Melbourne, Australia
868 United States (M Giles, B Fleisher, J Lewis, R Siderowf)
1970 Puerta de Hierro, Spain
857 United States (M Giles, T Kite, A Miller, L Wadkins)
1972 Olivos GC, Argentina
865 United States (B Crenshaw, M Giles, M Hayes, M West)
1974 Campo de Golf, Dominica
888 United States (G Burns, G Koch, J Pate, C Strange)
1976 Penina, Portugal
892 Great Britain (J Davies, I Hutcheon, M Kelley, S Martin)
1978 Pacific Harbour, Fiji
873 United States (R Clampett, J Cook, S Hoch, J Sigel)
1980 Pinehurst, United States
848 United States (H Sutton, J Holtgrieve, B Tway, J Sigel)
1982 Lausanne, Switzerland
859 United States (N Crosby, B Lewis, J Holtgrieve, J Sigel)

WOMEN'S WORLD AMATEUR TEAM CHAMPIONSHIP (ESPIRITO SANTO TROPHY)

1964 St Germain, France
588 France (C Lacoste, B Varangot, C Cros)
1966 Mexico City CC
580 United States (M Boddie, S Hamlin, A Quast-Welts)
1968 Victoria GC, Australia
616 United States (J Bastanchury, S Hamlin, A Quast-Welts)
1970 Club de Campo, Spain
598 United States (J Bastanchury, C Hill, M Wilkinson)
1972 Hindu CC, Argentina
583 United States (L Baugh, J Bastanchury-Booth, MA Budke)
1974 Campo de Golf, Dominica
620 United States (C Hill, D Massey, C Semple)
1976 Vilamoura, Portugal
605 United States (D Horton, N Lopez, D Massey)
1978 Pacific Harbour, Fiji
596 Australia (L Goggin, E Kennedy, J Lock)
1980 Pinehurst No 2, United States
588 United States (J Inkster, P Rizzo, C Semple)
1982 Geneva, Switzerland
579 United States (J Inkster, K Baker, A Benz)

WORLD MATCH-PLAY CHAMPIONSHIP

(at Wentworth)

1964 Arnold Palmer (US) bt Neil Coles 2 & 1
1965 Gary Player (S Africa) bt Peter Thomson (Australia) 3 & 2
1966 Gary Player (S Africa) bt Jack Nicklaus (US) 6 & 4
1967 Arnold Palmer (US) bt Peter Thomson (Australia) 2 holes
1968 Gary Player (S Africa) bt Bob Charles (NZ) 1 hole
1969 Bob Charles (NZ) bt Gene Littler (US) at 37th
1970 Jack Nicklaus (US) bt Lee Trevino (US) 2 & 1
1971 Gary Player (S Africa) bt Jack Nicklaus (US) 5 & 4
1972 Tom Weiskopf (US) bt Lee Trevino (US) 4 & 2
1973 Gary Player (S Africa) bt Graham Marsh (Australia) at 40th
1974 Hale Irwin (US) bt Gary Player (S Africa) 3 & 1
1975 Hale Irwin (US) bt Al Geiberger (US) 4 & 2
1976 David Graham (Australia) bt Hale Irwin (US) at 38th
1977 Graham Marsh (Australia) bt Raymond Floyd (US) 5 & 3
1978 Isao Aoki (Japan) bt Simon Owen (NZ) 3 & 2
1979 Bill Rogers (US) bt Isao Aoki (Japan) 1 hole
1980 Greg Norman (Australia) bt Sandy Lyle (GB) 1 hole
1981 Severiano Ballesteros (Spain) bt Ben Crenshaw (US) 1 hole
1982 Severiano Ballesteros (Spain) bt Sandy Lyle (GB) at 37th
1983 Greg Norman (Australia) bt Nick Faldo (GB) 3 & 2

Greg Norman (Australia).

Harry Vardon (England) in 1924.

JOHN BALL

Born December 24, 1861 Died 1940

Open champion 1890 Amateur champion 1888-90-92-94-99, 1907-10-12

John Ball was the first amateur and the first Englishman to win the Open Championship. He had two rounds of 82 at Prestwick in 1890, beating Willie Fernie, of Troon, and Archie Simpson, of Carnoustie, by three strokes. His first appearance had been at the age of 15 when he finished sixth, well ahead of many leading professionals.

It was in the Amateur Championship, however, that he achieved immortal fame, winning it no less than eight times between 1888 and 1912. His successes could well have run into double figures but he served in the Cheshire Yeomanry during the Boer war and did not compete in the championships of 1900-01-02.

Ball learned his golf at the Royal Liverpool club, Hoylake, being the son of the owner of the old Royal Hotel, close to the present 17th green. In the early years of his life, it was still a race course, the Royal Liverpool club not being founded until 1869.

This was the year of the birth of Harold Hilton, another famous Royal Liverpool club member who, as an amateur, won the Open Championship twice, in 1892 and 1897, and the Amateur Championship four times.

These noble golf links were a fine training ground for Ball and in his book *Golf Between Two Wars*, Bernard Darwin wrote: 'The beauty of any particular player's style must, like his exact place in the golfing firmament, be a matter of individual feeling, and I can only say that I have derived greater aesthetic and emotional pleasure from watching Mr Ball than from any other spectacle in any game'.

A reserved, even shy man, Ball's classic style stood him in good stead in many close finishes, two of his Amateur Championship victories being in finals that went to extra holes.

Ball's last Amateur Championship was in 1921 at Hoylake. He was then 60, the Americans had come over in force but he still reached the fifth round and remarked: 'If only a storm of wind and rain would sweep across the links from the Welsh hills, I still feel I could beat all of them again'. Instead the sun blazed down, he was beaten and retired to farm in North Wales.

SEVERIANO BALLESTEROS

Born April 9, 1957

Open champion 1979 Masters champion 1980-83

Severiano Ballesteros was 19 years old and largely unknown in Europe, let alone the world, when in 1976 he led the field for the first three rounds of the Open Championship at Royal Birkdale. In the end he tied second with Jack Nicklaus, six strokes behind Johnny Miller, but such was the freedom and daring of his shot-making that no one doubted that a star had been born.

Three years later he won the Open at Royal Lytham and St Annes, the first Spaniard and only the second continental (Arnaud Massy, of France, in 1907 was the first) to become champion. Within the year he celebrated his 23rd birthday with a 66 in the first round of the Masters at Augusta National and three days later was champion. He was the first continental professional to be entitled to wear the club's exclusive green jacket and only the second non-American, Gary Player being the first. Three years later, in 1983, Ballesteros won the Masters for a second time.

Yet it was just as much as an international golfer that Ballesteros made his reputation. Though he could have played the American tour fulltime had he so wished—his first victory on the US circuit was in the Greater Greensboro in 1978—Ballesteros preferred not to commit himself.

He was loath to cut his ties completely with the European circuit, his training ground since joining the tour in 1974. He liked to be able to take periodic rests at his Santander home in northern Spain and it appealed to him to win in as many countries as possible. Nor was he short of invitations.

Consequently Ballesteros' lengthening list of victories

have bridged countries of many different languages—from Holland, where the Dutch Open in 1976 provided him with his first win of importance—to France, Switzerland, Japan, New Zealand, Kenya, Germany, Sweden, Australia, all in addition of course to those in Spain, America and many in Britain. He finished leading money winner in Europe for three successive years, beginning in 1976.

His fame did much for golf in Spain, for whom in 1976 and 1977 he helped to win the World Cup. He won the World Match-Play Championship at Wentworth in 1981 and 1982 and it was almost certainly because of him that the Great Britain and Ireland Ryder Cup team was extended in 1979 so that it could also include continental players.

Wrangles over appearance money cast something of a cloud over Ballesteros' career at one point and his belief in his rights together with his single-minded determination were as formidable off the golf course as they were on it.

But his golf has won admiration everywhere he has played. His glorious swing, generating great power, provides tireless watching. It has not been in his Latin blood to play safe and while it may have taken him to some unlikely places on many courses, such are his powers of recovery and so delicate his touch on and around the greens that he has been able to prosper where most would have perished.

JAMES BRAID

Born February 6, 1870 Died 1950
Open champion 1901-05-06-08-10

The name of James Braid is always linked with his two contemporaries, JH Taylor and Harry Vardon. They were known as the Great Triumvirate, ruling as they did the Open Championship over a span lasting 20 years. Between 1894 and 1914, there were only five years when one of them did not win.

Braid was the oldest of the three but only by a matter of months. He was, nevertheless, the last of them to win the Open. For by the time of his first triumph, at Muirfield in 1901, both Vardon and Taylor had been crowned three times. Once he had 'broken through', there was no stopping Braid. By 1910 he had become the first man to have won the championship five times, a feat equalled by Vardon the following year, by Taylor in 1913 and then passed by Vardon in 1914. Since then only Peter Thomson, of Australia, and Tom Watson, of America, have succeeded in taking the title five times.

A Scot by birth, Braid left school at the age of 13 and began his working life as a joiner. Of humble background, his father being a ploughman, Braid was not encouraged to play golf, though he did so with some modest success as an amateur. He turned professional at the age of 23, when a friend urged him to take up an appointment as a club maker in London.

This enabled him to play golf both at the weekends and in the summer evenings and his aggressive style of play soon began to get results, even though he did not once break 80—and in one round not even 90—when he entered his first Open Championship at Sandwich in 1894, the first incidentally to be held outside Scotland.

However he had made a start and the following year halved a match with Taylor, who had just won the Open two years running. A golfer, consequently of some stature, he was appointed professional at Romford, Essex, where he remained for eight years before moving to Walton Heath, an association that was to last him the rest of his days.

Professional tournaments were rare in Braid's day and he earned much of his living through exhibition and challenge matches. However he was the first British Match-Play champion, an event he won four times and he also won the French Open in 1910.

A man who was once described as 'hitting the ball with a divine fury', Braid admitted to going to bed a short driver and getting up the next morning a long one. 'It was then, and still is, the greatest golfing mystery that I have ever come across'.

Braid was also a golf course architect of some standing. Together with Taylor and Willie Auchterlonie he was made an honorary member of the Royal and Ancient in 1950, the first professionals to be so honoured.

HENRY COTTON

Born January 26, 1907
Open champion 1934-37-48

Henry Cotton's three Open Championship victories have set him apart from all other British golfers since the first world war. That at Sandwich in 1934 stemmed an American tide that had swept remorselessly over the event since 1923. It was his misfortune that the second world war came at a time when he was still in his prime.

Though not a naturally gifted golfer, Cotton climbed to the top through application, dedication and character. He was a wonderfully straight driver and it was often hard to tell whether he had driven down the right hand side of the fairway or the left, so straight was he. His iron play was hardly less exact and if his putting appeared to be in not quite the same class, it was probably because he was putting for more birdies than anyone else.

From the very beginning Cotton did everything in style. In the Open Championship at Sandwich in 1934 he scored 67,

65 in the first two rounds (the second of which gave the name to the Dunlop ball) and led by 10 strokes after three rounds. Nervous and sick before the final round, his golf was in danger of total collapse before he recovered on the inward half and won by five strokes.

Cotton's final round of 71 in torrential rain and on a waterlogged course at Carnoustie in the 1938 Open, when the Americans were again over in force, was among the greatest of his career. While at Muirfield in 1948 he set a course record of 66 in the second round—appropriately regal golf since King George VI was among the gallery.

Three times British Match-Play champion, and three times runner-up, Cotton also won many of the continental championships. He played three times in the Ryder Cup, once as playing captain, and was non-playing captain in a match Great Britain and Ireland nearly won at Wentworth in 1953.

He had something in common with Walter Hagen, who had led the emancipation of professional golf. Of lively, enquiring mind, he had the ability to mix with princes and paupers alike. Cotton exploited his many talents to the full, even appearing on the same bill at the London Coliseum as Nellie Wallace. On a darkened stage, hands shoes and golf balls treated with luminous paint, he went through a 15-minute routine.

He served for some years as professional at Waterloo, in Belgium, and also at Cannes in the South of France. When he set up a golf school in Monte Carlo, his millionaire pupils drove golf balls into the sea. Invalided out of the RAF during the 1939-45 war, he raised considerable sums of money for the Red Cross, in recognition of which he was made an MBE.

In his 50th year Cotton tied sixth in the 1956 Open Championship at Hoylake and he was 70 when he competed for the last time at Turnberry in 1977. Spurred on by his wife, Toots, he wrote as many books as he designed courses, his pride and joy being Penina on Portugal's Algarve coast, his home for many years.

WALTER HAGEN

Born December 21, 1892 Died 1969
Open champion 1922-24-28-29 US Open champion 1914-19 American PGA champion 1921-24-25-26-27

It has been said that every professional golfer should, as he collects his cheque at the end of a tournament, say a silent vote of thanks to Walter Hagen. A flamboyant, even extroverted American, he was the first purely tournament professional and pioneered the standard of living enjoyed today.

Hagen always claimed that he never wanted to be a

Walter Hagen (United States).

millionaire, 'only to live like one'. It was one of the many famous sayings attributed to him, others that spring to mind being that one should always take time off to 'smell the roses', and of an opponent who had retired early: 'He may be in bed but he's not sleeping'.

Professional golfers were regarded as second-class citizens until Hagen began to exert his influence. When not admitted to the clubhouse at an Open Championship at Deal, he hired a Rolls Royce and a butler and had champagne and caviar served to him outside the front door.

When he found a similar restriction at Troon, he politely declined to enter the clubhouse for the presentation and instead invited spectators to the inn where he was staying, for a drink. Thus when the Inverness club in Toledo opened its doors to professionals at the US Open in 1920, Hagen was the first to recognise the gesture, organising a collection among his fellow players and presenting the club with a grandfather clock bearing the inscription:

> God measures men by what they are
> Not what they in wealth possess.
> This vibrant message chimes afar
> The voice of Inverness.

If there was a secret to Hagen's success as a golfer, it was his temperament. Though he expected to hit only two or three really good shots in any one round, he regarded nothing as impossible and it bred within his opponents the feeling that he was invincible.

This was best illustrated in his four consecutive victories in the American PGA, all by match-play. Against that country's very best players he won 22 successive matches.

Hagen did nothing by halves. In 1928 he lost a challenge match against Archie Compston, a formidable match-player, by 18 and 17 over 72 holes but went straight to Hoylake and won the Open Championship for a second time.

His first appearance, in 1920, had caused less impact. He finished 26 strokes behind the winner, George Duncan, at Deal but vowed that he would 'be back'. He was. Two years later he triumphed at Sandwich, thereby becoming the first American-born champion. It was typical of him that he should promptly give the whole of his prize money to his caddie.

Hagen brought colour to golf in many ways, not least in the style of his dress. He exchanged the jacket popular among his predecessors for a pullover or cardigan and introduced black and white shoes, still fashionable today.

He was captain, in 1937, of the first American Ryder Cup team to win on British soil, having been a member of every side since the inaugural match in 1921.

BEN HOGAN

Born August 13, 1912

Open champion 1953 US Open champion 1948-50-51-53 Masters champion 1951-53 American PGA champion 1946-48

Ben Hogan was 17 when he turned professional, 25 before he won his first tournament and 33 before he won his first major championship, the American PGA at Portland, Oregon, defeating Porky Oliver by six and four in the final.

These bald facts are worth relating because they illustrate that success did not come easily even to a man who was certainly the greatest player of his time and also one of the greatest of all time. Few have sought such perfection, let alone attained it. Practice indeed made perfect.

Hogan was only two months short of his 36th birthday when he won the US Open Championship for the first time at Riviera, California, in 1948, a year in which he collected his second PGA. But just as his career was coming to full bloom, so fate struck him a near mortal blow.

In February 1949 he was involved in a fearful car crash, pinned in the wreckage for 90 minutes before his mangled body and legs could be released and taken to hospital for extensive surgery. It was hard to believe that he would ever play golf again.

Not only did he play again but he emerged, if anything, a greater golfer than he had been before, going on to win the US Open on three more occasions, in 1950, 1951 and

1953, the Masters in 1951 and 1953 and the Open Championship in 1953. It was a staggering achievement for a man who was never again completely fit.

Only three other players, Gene Sarazen, Jack Nicklaus and Gary Player, have triumphed in these four major professional championships and Hogan is the only one to have taken three of them, the Masters, US Open and Open Championship in the same year, 1953. A clash of dates with the Open prevented his going for the Grand Slam in the PGA.

Hogan played no competitive golf at all in 1949 as he recuperated from his injuries but in January 1950 he made a tentative return in the Los Angeles Open and at once tied with Sam Snead before losing the play-off. Then he tied again in the US Open at Merion and this time won the play-off.

In 1951 he successfully defended at Oakland Hills, so savagely difficult that he vowed that he would 'bring this monster to its knees' and did so with a 67 in the final round. But 1953 was, of course, his finest. It was the only time he entered for the Open Championship, at Carnoustie.

A second victory in the Masters and a fourth in the US Open persuaded him that he could never be regarded as the complete golfer until he had mastered British conditions as well. He arrived two weeks in advance, learned the course in all its capricious moods and proceeded to destroy it, each round being lower than the one before 73, 71, 70, 68.

That final round has remained firmly etched in the memory of all who saw it for his driving and approach play, allied to his ruthless determination, were in a class of their own. This proved to be his last 'major' for though in 1955 he again tied for the US Open, he lost the play-off to Jack Fleck, a club professional.

Nevertheless in 14 consecutive US Opens until 1960 and in 14 consecutive Masters until 1956, Hogan was always in the top 10 and 18 times in the first four.

BOBBY JONES

Born March 17, 1902 Died 1971
Open champion 1926-27-30 Amateur champion 1930
US Open champion 1923-26-29-30
US Amateur champion 1924-25-27-28-30

Immediately after Bobby Jones had completed his fourth round of the Open Championship at Hoylake in 1930, he sat in the lounge of the Royal Liverpool club totally drained, needing both hands to steady the glass in his hand.

Declining rounds of 70, 72, 74 and 75 had given him a total of 291 but in those days the leaders did not go out last and Leo Diegel, Macdonald Smith, two other Americans, and Archie Compston all had a chance of overtaking him. None of them did but as Jones waited he murmured, almost to himself, that he would 'never, never do it again'.

A few weeks earlier he had won the Amateur Championship for the only time at St Andrews—with its 18-hole matches he always maintained that this was the hardest championship of all—and for the first time the Grand Slam (or Impregnable Quadrilateral as Jones liked to call it) was a realistic possibility.

At Interlachen in the US Open and Merion in the US Amateur, he duly completed his conquest of these four major championships. But the frayed state of his nerves as he awaited the outcome of the Open Championship at Hoylake, reflected the strain he was always under.

There were days, his close friend OB Keeler disclosed, when Jones could scarcely eat until the day's play was done, when he could hardly button his shirt collar (in those days it was the fashion to wear a tie even when playing golf) for fear of making himself sick. He would often lose a stone in weight during a single championship.

Finally it was too much to bear. Jones was 28 when he completed the Grand Slam. At once he retired and 'never, never did it again'.

Yet his supremacy while he reigned was absolute. Though something of a child prodigy in that he was 14 when he won the Georgia State Amateur, only 16 when he took the Southern Amateur and 17 when he was runner-up in both the Canadian Open and US Amateur, he was nevertheless 21 before he at last won his first major, the US Open at Inwood, New York, in 1923.

He never looked back. In eight years he collected 13 major championships, a total since surpassed only by Jack Nicklaus. Between 1922 and 1930—nine years—he not only won the US Open four times but he was runner-up four times as well.

In his five US Amateur Championship victories between 1924 and 1930, Jones's average margin in the semi-finals and finals were nine and eight. In five Walker Cup matches, he won his singles over 36 holes by an average of eight and seven.

When he first played in the Open Championship, at St Andrews in 1921, he tore up his card in frustration. Yet he came to love the Old Course as nowhere else and when in 1958 he came over as captain of the American team in the inaugural Eisenhower trophy, he was given the Freedom of the Burgh of St Andrews.

Jones never played other than with hickory clubs. When he retired he helped in the design of Augusta National and thereby established one of the show-pieces of golf, the Masters.

Tragically his last years were made a misery by a crippling muscular disease though he bore it with the same dignity he had borne his many triumphs.

BOBBY LOCKE

Born November 20, 1917
Open champion 1949-50-52-57

Bobby Locke, a South African, was proof that golf is not a game of 'how' but rather one of 'how many'. In other words, he could still return a very decent score, even when playing badly, and that undoubtedly is the hallmark of the very best golfer.

He was unusual in that he struck all his shots with draw, even his putts, but he still had wonderful control of the ball and was one of the most deadly putters of all time. However, this was born of temperament as well as method. A methodical golfer, Locke never allowed himself to be rushed for he knew that that would destroy his rhythm. On occasions, he was accused of slow play, but he was always the most courteous of players, carefully turned out and, at the height of his career, a familiar figure in his white cap and plus fours.

Though best known for his four Open Championship victories—he was the first man to record as many since the days of the Triumvirate, Vardon, Braid and Taylor—Locke also had considerable success in America.

He was persuaded to go there by Sam Snead, whom he had beaten 12 times in 16 challenge matches in South Africa. In his first tournament, the 1947 Masters, Locke finished 15th. From there on he built the extraordinary record of winning six of his next 12 events, being second twice and never worse than seventh. He was the year's second leading money winner.

In 1948 he played 25 American tournaments and though this time he won only two, he was runner-up five times and on only three occasions failed to finish among the top ten. Yet his relationship with Americans was never an easy one and instead he turned his attentions to Britain where he had first played as an amateur, with some success before the war.

Locke had finished second to Snead in the Open at St Andrews in 1946 and his first victory was at Royal St George's in 1949 where he beat Harry Bradshaw, of Ireland, in a play-off. In one round a shot of Bradshaw's had come to rest in a broken bottle and, not knowing what to do and in the absence of a ruling, he played the ball as it lay, smashing the bottle in the process.

Locke had the enviable ability to put a bad hole immediately out of his mind. When he successfully defended his Open title at Troon in 1950, he took six at the short fifth. But he more than wiped the slate clean with four birdies in the next six holes. His temperament was quite unflappable.

Max Faulkner denied him a hat-trick of wins at Royal Portrush in 1951 but at Lytham a year later Locke prevailed for a third time. His last success was at St Andrews in 1957 when, with 'three for it' from a matter of inches on the final green, he forgot that he had had to re-mark his ball a putter blade to one side and putted from the wrong place. No penalty was subsequently imposed.

There was total justice in the decision but Locke, nine times South African Open champion (twice as an amateur) never played golf in plus fours again.

TOM MORRIS JUNIOR

Born April 20, 1851 Died 1875
Open champion 1868-69-70-72

Young Tom Morris is the only man who, by his very excellence, brought the Open Championship to a halt. His third successive victory at Prestwick in 1870 meant that he won the handsome red leather championship belt outright and with no alternative prize immediately available, the host and organising club suspended competition for 12 months.

However by the following year approaches had been made to the Royal and Ancient and to the Honourable Company of Edinburgh Golfers, whose home was then at Musselburgh rather than Muirfield, as it is now, and for the next 22 years these three clubs combined to both run and stage the championship. They also subscribed to the present championship cup which Young Tom promptly won, making a sequence of four in a row.

This still stands as a record, as does his age, 17, when he first won the title in 1868, succeeding his father, Old Tom, which is also without parallel. The following year they finished first and second respectively and that, too, is a feat unlikely to be repeated.

Together then, father and son very much dominated the championship's early years for Old Tom himself took possession of the belt four times before his young son began to assert himself.

Young Tom became the more legendary figure, not least because he achieved so much in so short a time. He won £5, then a princely sum, in a challenge match at the age of 13 and was fourth behind his father in the Open at the age of 16.

His father was once quoted as saying that while he always felt capable of handling Allan Robertson—a great figure in the game but one who died just before the birth of the Open—'I could never cope wi' Wee Tommy'. It was indeed tragic that he should die so young, 24.

Married only a year earlier, his young wife had died in childbirth. The news reached Young Tom as he was about to sail from North Berwick to be at her side. He had been playing a foursomes match with his father. Within three months Young Tom was dead as well, some said of a broken heart, and a memorial in St Andrews cathedral bears the inscription:

'Deeply regretted by numerous friends and all golfers, he thrice in succession won the championship belt and held it without rivalry and yet without envy, his many amiable qualities being no less acknowledged than his golfing achievements'.

A fierce if not entirely elegant hitter of the ball—he was known even to break his hickory shafted clubs in the midst of his preliminary waggle—Young Tom's most commanding Open victory was his third when he had no less than 12 strokes to spare, second only to his father's 13 strokes in 1862.

Over the 36 holes that were played in those days—three rounds of a 12-hole course—it was a huge margin and his total of 149, one over fours with the gutty ball, a remarkable achievement. It included a three at the first hole, which measured well in excess of 500 yards, though whether he sank a putt or an approach has been lost in time.

JACK NICKLAUS

Born January 21, 1940
Open champion 1966-70-78 US Open champion 1962-67-72-80
Masters champion 1963-65-66-72-75
American PGA champion 1963-71-73-75-80
US Amateur champion 1959-61

Jack Nicklaus has always maintained that no record is sacrosanct and that the many he has set in his glittering career, will one day be beaten. Even so there must be limits for it is hard to imagine the calibre of golfer it would take to surpass his many achievements.

Only three other men, Gene Sarazen, Ben Hogan and Gary Player, have at some time or other won the two Open Championships, the Masters and the PGA. Nicklaus has completed the set three times. Bobby Jones held the previous record of 13 major championships. Nicklaus has won 19, 17 of them as a professional.

He holds the record of the most victories in the Masters (five) and jointly holds the record of the most wins in both the PGA (five) and the US Open (four). His 69 victories on the American tour since 1962 have been exceeded only by Sam Snead's 84 and he is the first man whose winnings have passed four million dollars.

It has been Nicklaus's ability to move into another gear, in the major championships, that has been so impressive. Apart from his 17 victories as a professional, he has been second or tied second 18 times and been third or tied third nine times. That makes a total of 44 occasions in 88 consecutive appearances that he has finished in the top three.

As an amateur, Nicklaus was still only 20 when he finished runner-up to Arnold Palmer in the US Open at Cherry Hills in 1960. The following year, still an amateur, he was equal fourth. When he turned professional in 1962, he spectacularly 'reserved' his first victory for the US Open at Oakmont, beating Arnold Palmer, who was then at the height of his career, in a play-off.

In 1963, only his second season, he became the youngest winner of the Masters (though Severiano Ballesteros has since claimed that distinction) and by the end of the year he was PGA champion as well. But it was not until 1966 that he completed his first 'set' of major championships, winning the Open at Muirfield.

It was on this course in the 1959 Walker Cup match that Nicklaus made his first appearance in Britain and such was the impression it made on him, he later named his course in Ohio, Muirfield Village, home each year of the Memorial tournament.

When he won his second Masters in 1965, setting a record total of 271 (subsequently equalled by Raymond Floyd) Bobby Jones remarked: 'Mr Nicklaus plays a game with which I am not familiar'. Nicklaus also has the lowest winning score (272) in the US Open, set at Baltusrol in 1980, where his opening round of 63 is another all-time championship 'low', equalled the same day by Tom Weiskopf and matching the 63 by Johnny Miller in the final round at Oakmont in 1973.

A golfer of great strength and deliberation. He frequently locks himself over a putt until you think he has become transfixed.

After some early unpopularity in America while he was in the process of de-throning the national hero, Palmer, Nicklaus has won acclaim all over the world, not only for his excellence but also for his generosity in defeat. His respect for the traditions of the game, notable in his support of the Open Championship in which he has finished in the first three 13 times in 22 attempts, has been largely responsible for the present standing of that event.

ARNOLD PALMER

Born September 10, 1929

Open champion 1961-62 US Open champion 1960
Masters champion 1958-60-62-64 US Amateur champion 1954

The explosion of interest golf enjoyed in the late 1950s and 60s owed a great deal to one man, Arnold Palmer. His aggressive way of playing the game, together with an easy, friendly disposition made him one of the heroes of American sporting history, his reputation spreading worldwide.

Two events in particular, the Masters in 1960 and the United States Open the same year, were the making of his reputation. Though Palmer had already won the Masters once, in 1958, it was his second victory that caught the imagination as he displayed a rare capacity for rising to the occasion under the severest pressure. Coming to the last three holes at Augusta National, Palmer needed three birdies to beat Ken Venturi. He got them, finishing 2, 3, 3 and at once gave birth to the now-legendary expression of a 'Palmer charge'.

A few months later he triumphed just as spectacularly in the US Open at Cherry Hills. After three rounds Palmer trailed Mike Souchak, the leader, by seven strokes. He was five behind Julius Boros and Dow Finsterwald, four behind Jack Nicklaus (then an amateur), three behind Jack Fleck and one behind Dutch Harrison. But Palmer, with that famous 'hitch of his pants' on the first tee, promptly drove the first green, a par four, had six birdies in seven holes, was out in 30, round in 65 and won by two strokes from Nicklaus. Surprisingly and sadly it was his only US Open victory, though he should have won again.

With nine holes to play at the Olympic club, San Francisco, in 1966, Palmer led Billy Casper by seven strokes but, after an outward half of 32, he took 39 to come home and was caught. Then in the play-off the following day he lost another lead, this time of two strokes after nine holes, Casper beating him with a 69 against a 73.

It was a reverse from which Palmer never recovered, though the initial damage had perhaps been done four years earlier at Oakmont, when he lost another play-off, this time to Nicklaus, who was in only his first year as a professional. He never entirely escaped his tormentor's shadow.

The American PGA was the only major championship to elude Palmer's clutches, but he had a good deal to do with the revival of the Open, which he first contested in its centenary year at St Andrews in 1960. Having already won the Masters and US Open that year he had the chance to equal Ben Hogan's three 'majors' in the same season.

Instead Palmer lost by a stroke to Kel Nagle, of Australia. However, he was back the following year at Royal Birkdale where he triumphed in heavy wind and rain, and he defended successfully at Troon in 1962 on a fast-running course that emphasised his ability to master any conditions.

Palmer was particularly at home at Augusta, where he won four times between 1958 and 1964 and was the first man whose tournament winnings exceeded one million dollars. Under the able management of Mark McCormack, Palmer also developed wide-ranging business interests, though his urge to play golf competitively has remained with him well beyond his 50th birthday.

That famous whip-lash at the top of his followthrough, big hands enveloping the grip of the club, the glove stuck carelessly in his hip pocket... they are all part of the Arnold Palmer legend. So much so that many people would prefer to see him remove his clubs from the boot of his car than watch another man complete a round of 67.

GARY PLAYER

Born November 1, 1935
Open champion 1959-68-74 US Open champion 1965
Masters champion 1961-74-78 American PGA champion 1962-72

Just as Vardon, Braid and Taylor were known as golf's Triumvirate, so Player, Nicklaus and Palmer were regarded in the 1960s and 70s as the game's Big Three. At 5ft 7in, Player was hardly big in size, but he was a man of remarkable determination. Other perhaps than Ben Hogan, from whom he drew much of his inspiration, no one has spent more hours on the practice ground and achieved so much when the odds were so heavily stacked against him.

It is doubtful if any golfer has flown the number of miles Player has done for, as a South African he always remained loyal to his home country, returning home whenever he could, to his farm and his horses. His ability to fall asleep almost before his aeroplane left the runway and remain asleep until it landed, was one of his most valuable assets.

Player is justly proud of his record as a 'global' golfer. With Hogan, Nicklaus and Sarazen he is one of only four men to have conquered the quadrilateral of the four major professional championships. He has the distinction of having won the Open Championship in three different decades (1959, 1968 and 1974). He has been Australian Open champion seven times, South African champion 13 times and won the World Match-Play championship five times.

A recovery he made in the latter, when he stood seven down with 17 to play against Tony Lema and came back to win, was typical of his courage—something he showed from the very beginning of his career. There were so many technical faults in his swing and grip when he first came to Britain in 1955 that no one detected in him a future champion.

But his intense dedication, willingness to learn and obsession for building up his golfing muscles soon began to bring results. In 1958 he was second in the US Open at Southern Hills and the following year won his first Open at Muirfield after being eight strokes behind at the half-way stage and still four behind going into the final round.

Player's breakthrough in America came in 1961 when he took the Masters from under the nose of Palmer, who was then at the height of his powers. It had looked like being Palmer's third victory in four years but Player got 'up and down' from a bunker beside the 18th green whereas Palmer took another four shots after being in the same bunker and lost by a stroke.

Player was also leading American money winner that year and in 1962 added the PGA to his growing collection of titles, ironically having been at the point of giving up what he described in his book, *Grand Slam Golf*, as 'this ridiculous life'.

His US Open victory at Bellerive in 1965 completed his set of the four major championships and perhaps the only disappointment in his career was that he did not win it again. It has been the only one he has not won twice.

There was no more spectacular victory than that in the Masters of 1978 when he came from seven strokes behind with a final round of 64, playing the inward half in 30. Nor was there a more complete one than his third Open Championship victory at Royal Lytham in 1974. He led throughout, mastering the larger 1.68inch ball, which was in compulsory use for the first time, so completely in some heavy weather that he was the only man to break 70, which he did, not once, but twice.

As a South African, Player was often the target of anti apartheid demonstrations, once needing an armed bodyguard on the course. But he always handled these difficult moments diplomatically and calmly and without effect to his golf.

Gary Player (South Africa).

ALLAN ROBERTSON

Born 1815 Died 1859

Allan Robertson was in one way responsible for the birth of the Open Championship. By his death at the age of 44, the game of golf in Scotland was deprived of its best player. It was in an attempt to find a successor that, the following year, on October 17, 1860, the Prestwick club held the inaugural championship. Eight professionals participated and Willie Park took the red leather belt—later to be won outright by Young Tom Morris—with a score of 174 for the 36 holes.

Robertson was a contemporary of Young Tom's father, Old Tom Morris. A native of St Andrews, he was the most accomplished of all the artisan golfers of that city and was the first player to use irons from the fairway successfully.

It is also said that he was the first man to break 80 round the Old Course, scoring 79 the year before his death. His figures, remarkable considering he was using the feathery ball, were: 4,4,4, 5,5,6, 4,4,4, (40) 4,3,5, 6,4,5, 5,4,3 (39).

In those days a lot of golf was by foursomes match-play and legend had it that Robertson and Old Tom were defeated only once, and then only in the second of a three-leg match against the brothers Dunn, of Musselburgh.

The stake was the then enormous one of £400. Robertson and Morris won the first at St Andrews, lost at Musselburgh but in the decider at North Berwick and watched by a vast crowd they came back from four down with eight to play winning on the last green, to preserve their record.

This successful combination by the two men on the golf course was a happy example of how differences off it can be forgotten. The Robertson family had been makers of clubs and balls for many years and when Allan took over the shop close by the 18th green at St Andrews, Tom Morris joined him as assistant. Together they produced the best part of 2,500 featheries a year—good going since manufacture was a slow and laborious business—but differences arose when Old Tom began to take an interest in the new gutta percha ball. Robertson saw this as a major threat to his livelihood and they went their separate ways.

If Robertson pioneered iron play, not only with short pitches to the green but also with the longer approach shots, it was a fashion that did not catch on until Young Tom Morris proved its effectiveness some years after.

However, Robertson was undoubtedly the finest golfer of his time and those who subsequently saw Harry Vardon play golf as well were very much of the opinion that there was a distinct similarity of both style and elegance. No tribute can be higher than that.

GENE SARAZEN

Born February 27, 1902
Open champion 1932 US Open champion 1922-32
Masters champion 1935 American PGA champion 1922-23-33

Eugene Saraceni, the son of an Italian immigrant, changed his name to Gene Sarazen for fear he might be regarded as a violinist. He took to golf almost by chance, having contracted pleurisy when an apprenticed carpenter. He subsequently became the first man to win all four of the world's major professional championships.

The four-wood shot he holed for an albatross two at Augusta's 15th hole in the final round, which led to his tieing with Craig Wood in the 1935 Masters, then winning the play-off to complete the full house, has gone down in history as one of the most dramatic, if fortunate, strokes in the game.

Nor was it his last. In 1973, then aged 71 and making a nostalgic return visit to the Open Championship at Troon where he had first contested the event 50 years before (failing to qualify!), Sarazen holed in one at the postage stamp eighth. It was a shot caught by the television cameras and the following day at the same hole he sank a bunker shot for a two.

A beaming, olive-skinned man, even shorter in stature than Gary Player, Sarazen's distinguished career consequently spanned more than half a century. With Bobby Jones (1926 and 1930), Ben Hogan (1953), Lee Trevino (1971) and Tom Watson (1982) he achieved the rare feat of winning the Open Championships of Britain and America in the same year.

His first US Open victory came very early in his career. He was still only 20 when he won at Skokie, Illinois, in 1922, having entered the championship for experience more than anything, and sharing a dormitory with a number of other professionals. But he won the PGA the same year and defended it successfully in 1923, beating moreover Walter Hagen, who seemed almost invincible at match-play at this time.

Sarazen's failure to qualify for the Open Championship at Troon later the same year undermined his confidence. A dashing, aggressive player who seemed to just stand up to the ball and hit it, he suddenly became weighed down by technique.

When Sarazen returned again for the Open at Hoylake in 1924 he finished no higher than in a tie for 41st place and it was not until 1932, having by then finished runner-up to Hagen in 1928, that he finally succeeded, winning by five strokes from another American, Macdonald Smith, at Prince's, Sandwich.

Some two or three weeks later, Sarazen won the US Open

for a second time at Fresh Meadow, New York, possibly the greatest of his triumphs. Having played the first two rounds defensively and taking 74 and 76, he completed the last 28 holes in 100 strokes, including a last round of 66.

Such scoring was unheard of in those days and drew from Jones the comment that it was 'the finest competitive exhibition on record'. Twelve months later Sarazen won the PGA for a second time, 11 years after his first.

This was the last of his championship victories, though in 1933 he did finish only a stroke behind Densmore Shute in his defence of the Open Championship at St Andrews. It might have been very different had he not taken six at the short 11th where he failed to extricate himself from a bunker.

This was ironic for Sarazen's design and mastery of the sand iron transformed the game.

SAM SNEAD

Born May 27, 1912

Open champion 1946 Masters champion 1949-52-54
American PGA champion 1942-49-51

The only deficiency in Sam Snead's remarkable record over as long a period as any man has ever played golf competitively is that he never won the United States Open Championship. He won the last of his 84 tournaments on the American circuit, the Greater Greensboro Open in 1965, two months short of his 53rd birthday while in 1979 he beat his age, then 67, in the Quad Cities Open.

No man has made the game look quite so easy. Blessed with a body so supple that even into his sixties he could, while standing on one leg kick the lintel of a doorway with the other, Snead's fluent, easy swing was a total mastery of timing.

Twice he went tantalisingly close to that US Open that always eluded him. In 1939 at Philadelphia he came to the last hole leading the field. A par five would have been sufficient, though in those days the leaders did not go out last and there was no way he could have calculated it.

At all events he was bunkered beside the green in three, failed to get out first time and then took three putts. His eight left him in fifth place, two strokes behind Byron Nelson, Craig Wood and Densmore Shute, all of whom tied, Nelson winning the play-off.

Then in 1947 at St Louis, Snead did tie, holing a putt for a birdie on the last green to draw level with Lew Worsham. But 24 hours later he missed a putt of less than a yard on the same green in the play-off and lost by a stroke, 70 to Worsham's 69.

In 1949 he played the last nine holes at Medinah in 34 and failed to catch Cary Middlecoff by just one stroke. The accumulation of these near misses built a US Open block in Snead's mind.

It was a very different story in the Masters, he and Ben Hogan dominating the event between 1949 and 1954. Snead triumphed three times and Hogan twice. These were memorable times at Augusta and helped to make the tournament what it is today.

Snead played in three Open Championships, two more than Hogan, and won once, at St Andrews in 1946. As a member of the visiting American Ryder Cup side in 1937 he had finished 11th behind Henry Cotton at Carnoustie and in 1962 he was sixth behind Arnold Palmer at Troon.

British golfing conditions did not appeal to him—he once described it as 'camping out'—and his success at St Andrews lacked impact in the immediate aftermath of the second world war.

All Snead's victories in the PGA were at match-play. In the Ryder Cup, he was a member of seven American teams, and won all his singles except one, going down to Harry Weetman at Wentworth after being four up with six to play, in a match the Americans came to within a whisker of losing.

One of the more lasting impressions he made in Britain came in 1956 when he helped Ben Hogan to win the World Cup on the same Surrey course. He partnered Arnold Palmer, twice, and Jimmy Demaret to similar successes.

Putting difficulties marred the evening of Snead's career. Having found consolation in the croquet method, which was rather unkindly ruled illegal, he went 'side saddle' with his left and right hands far apart and such was his adaptability that he remained a force long after others would have retired.

J H TAYLOR

Born March 19, 1871 Died 1963
Open champion 1894-95-1900-09-13

John Henry Taylor was always known as 'JH'. He was the first of the celebrated Triumvirate to win the Open Championship, at Sandwich in 1894, lighting the way for his two contemporaries, Harry Vardon and James Braid. For 20 years they ruled supreme until the outbreak of the first world war in 1914.

Though not an educated man, leaving school indeed at the age of 11, Taylor was always keen to learn and became a natural leader, as well as a forceful speaker. He consequently had more than anyone else to do with the formation of the Professional Golfers' Association. Under his guidance, example and persuasion, professional golfers became far more respected people than they had been.

Taylor's character was first in evidence on the course. Though highly strung and inclined to treat every event in which he played as a battle, he was never better than when the elements were at their worst. He would pull down his cap, clamp his pipe between his teeth, plant his feet on the ground so firmly that not even a hurricane could shift him and then hit his shots through the wind as if none existed.

These qualities were particularly evident when Taylor won the fifth and last of his Open Championships at Hoylake in 1913. In appalling weather of wind and rain, he broke 80 every time and won by eight strokes from Ted Ray, a margin that still stands as the biggest since the days of the Morris's. Even he regarded this as his finest hour.

Born at Northam, on a hill overlooking Westward Ho! where he also died just short of his 93rd birthday, Taylor first came to prominence when he put up a good performance in the 1893 Open at Prestwick and when the championship moved to England for the first time the following year, he became the first English winner.

In 1895 he successfully defended the title at St Andrews and was only denied a hat-trick of victories at Muirfield the following year when he lost a play-off to Vardon.

It was not of course the only time that Vardon got the better of him, for in 1900 the two of them made a pilgrimage to Chicago for the United States Open and Vardon won by two strokes. It was the first time the championship cup was brought back across the Atlantic though it had of course been won before by ex-patriates.

However there was consolation for Taylor in that he won the Open Championship for a second time, and a third in all, at St Andrews and though Braid then 'moved in' with four victories between 1901 and 1908, Taylor was far from finished, as he proved at Deal in 1909.

At the age of 53 Taylor was still good enough to finish fifth in the 1924 Open at Hoylake when, counting his two qualifying rounds in which everybody had to participate, he had the lowest total of all, including that of Walter Hagen, the winner.

Though he had served for 40 years as professional at Royal Mid-Surrey, Taylor, already made an honorary member of the Royal and Ancient, ended his days back at Westward Ho! where, in 1957, he was made president of the Royal North Devon club. It was an honour he cherished more than any other.

PETER THOMSON

Born August 23, 1929
Open champion 1954-55-56-58-65

Peter Thomson is the finest Australian golfer of all time. Only Harry Vardon has exceeded his five Open Championship victories, winning six times. Thomson's five titles matched those by the two other members of the

Triumvirate, James Braid and JH Taylor, and has since been equalled by Tom Watson. His hat-trick of victories between 1954 and 1956 is without parallel this century.

Though he had considerable success elsewhere as well, winning the New Zealand Open nine times between 1950 and 1971 and his native Australian championship on three occasions, it was nevertheless in Britain that Thomson made his name.

It was a circuit towards which he was forced to turn because of the lack of tournament golf at that time in Australasia. A largely self-taught golfer from Melbourne, he nevetheless had an instinct for the game. He was always beautifully balanced, both at the top of the back-swing and at the completion of the followthrough and possessed a most enviable rhythm.

Nor was there anyone in the fifties who had such feel for the swift-running links courses. He was a master of the smaller 1.62 inch ball that was in use then and no one opposed more vigorously the introduction of the larger 1.68 inch ball.

Thomson, having turned professional at the age of 19, was still only 21 when he first came to Britain in 1951 and so quickly found his feet on a links that, at his first attempt, he finished equal sixth in the Open at Royal Portrush, eight strokes behind Max Faulkner, the last British winner until Tony Jacklin 18 years later.

Twelve months later Thomson was second to Bobby Locke, at Royal Lytham, equal second again in 1953 to Ben Hogan and therefore one of the least surprising winners when he triumphed at last at Royal Birkdale, which was introduced to the championship roster, in 1954.

Thus began three years of total domination, briefly interrupted by Bobby Locke at St Andrews in 1957, before Thomson made it four out of five at Lytham after a tie with David Thomas.

As Thomson had also finished runner-up to Locke at St Andrews, he did not finish out of the first two in eight consecutive years. Admittedly the Americans were more notable for their absence than presence but if Thomson needed proof of his ability against the highest class of opposition, he got it in 1965.

Back at Birkdale, the scene of his first victory, he won for the fifth and last time, beating among others Tony Lema, the holder, Jack Nicklaus and Arnold Palmer.

Though he was no great lover of golf in America, where he had of course to play with the big ball, Thomson nevertheless competed there with some success. He was once fourth in the US Open, fifth in the Masters and won the 1956 Dallas Open.

He twice partnered Kel Nagle to victory in the Canada Cup, later to become the World Cup, and continued to win numerous tournaments in Britain, notably the PGA Match-Play Championship four times.

Later Thomson became instrumental in the development of the Far Eastern circuit. A man with a keen intellectual mind, he developed interests in golf writing, broadcasting and golf course architecture and for his multiple services to the game he was made an MBE.

LEE TREVINO

Born December 1, 1939

Open champion 1971-72 US Open champion 1968-71
American PGA champion 1974

It would of course be an exaggeration to say that 'no one' had ever heard of Lee Trevino when he first won the United States Open Championship at Oak Hill, New York, in 1968. But it was his first victory on the American tour and a spectacular one at that, since he became the first man to beat par in every round (69,68,69,69).

Thus was launched one of the most engaging and amusing golfers of all time; one who, through an incessant flow of banter and wit, would alternately have galleries doubling up with mirth and then roaring their applause for some stroke of golfing genius. It was a rare mix: a natural comedian one moment and a professional of total concentration the next.

A Mexican of humble origin, Trevino learned to play the hard way. He was what was called a 'hustler', one who had to gamble on his ability to hit a golf ball just to make ends meet. He did not necessarily even have to use a golf club. He was more than a match for many when he handicapped himself by knocking the ball round with a taped up bottle, throwing the ball up and then volleying it.

Such an eye for a ball served him splendidly through his colourful career. Beginning in 1968, the year of that first US Open victory, he finished among the top ten American money winners for each of the next eight seasons, heading the list in 1970.

Trevino's outstanding year was 1971 when, in the space of three weeks, he won the American Open, the Canadian Open and the British Open. Twice, moreover, he had had to withstand the additional strain of play-offs. At Merion he had tied with Jack Nicklaus and at Montreal with Art Wall.

This latter play-off delayed Trevino's arrival at Royal Birkdale but the only signs of weariness he showed came at the very last gasp. Having led or jointly led from first to last, he took seven at the 17th and needed a birdie four at the 18th to resist the persistent attentions of the popular little Formosan, Lu Liang Huan, universally known as 'Mr Lu'.

Only Bobby Jones, Gene Sarazen and Ben Hogan had previously taken the two Open Championships of Britain and

America in the same year but Trevino's method, with his open stance and shoulder alignment, gave him a left-to-right control of the ball ideally suited to British conditions.

He liked nothing better than a good strong wind blowing across the course but in very peaceful conditions, he successfully defended the title at Muirfield in 1972, thanks largely to his holing three chip shots and one bunker shot in his four rounds.

The last of them, at the 17th hole on the final afternoon, so unnerved Tony Jacklin, his partner, that the British player took three putts, and lost a title which Trevino had told him was 'all yours' as they walked up the fairway.

A back injury, brought on when he was struck by lightning while sheltering during a thunderstorm, hampered Trevino in recent years, but he has remained in great demand all over the world for he brings considerable colour, as well as class to the game.

HARRY VARDON

Born May 9, 1870 Died 1937

Open champion 1896-98-99-1903-11-14 US Open champion 1900

The story is no doubt apocryphal but it was said of Harry Vardon that his greatest hazards in a round of golf lay in his having to play out of the divots he had made in his previous round. Apocryphal or not, it said much for the legendary accuracy and precision of a man who had a profound influence on the game.

Though some players, notably Jack Nicklaus, play with the interlocking grip and a very few with the double-handed grip (all ten fingers and thumbs on the club) the Vardon grip, with the little finger of the right hand overlapping the first finger of the left, is the most widely taught and used.

Vardon also swung the club on a much more upright plane than his predecessors had done and no less a judge than Bernard Darwin once wrote: 'I do not think anyone who saw him in his prime will disagree as to this, that a greater golfing genius is inconceivable'.

His six Open Championships, still unequalled, are testimony. For though James Braid and JH Taylor have very special places in the game's history, Vardon was the most celebrated of the Triumvirate. By sheer example, winning tournaments and breaking records almost everywhere he played, he opened up whole new horizons.

Born in Jersey, Vardon turned professional on the advice of his brother, moving in turn from Ripon to Bury, to Ganton and ultimately to South Herts, a club with which his name is always linked after service lasting more than 30 years.

Vardon's impact on the Open Championship was not immediate. Victory came at his fourth attempt, at Muirfield in 1896, and it was with the gutty ball that he was said to be at his best. Altogether he won with it on three occasions, the others being at Prestwick in 1898 and Sandwich in 1899.

Most of the time he carried both a spare driver and a spare brassie because of a hickory shaft's inclination to break. His clubs were light in weight and he would sometimes even use a ladies' set. But he was a long driver, the result more of timing than any noticeable aggression.

Such was Vardon's reputation that in 1900 he accepted an invitation to tour America, where the game was still in its infancy. Appropriately he won the US Open, beating JH Taylor by two strokes at Chicago, but his long absence from Britain affected his health.

When he won the Open Championship for a fourth time at Prestwick in 1903 he nearly collapsed more than once and finally had to go to a sanatorium where he happily made an almost complete recovery.

But it was not until 1911 that he gained his fifth success. Taken to a play-off by Arnaud Massy, of France, at Sandwich, Vardon so dominated the 36 holes that Massy conceded the title with one hole still to play.

Two years later he returned to America, he and Ted Ray losing in a play-off for the US Open at Brookline to a young amateur, Francis Ouimet. It proved to be the most significant result in American golfing history.

Vardon's sixth and last Open Championship victory came in 1914 at Prestwick, the third time he had won there. Vardon was then 44. The first world war may therefore have denied him even more success for at the age of 50 he was still good enough to finish second to Ted Ray in the 1920 US Open at Inverness. It was 50 years precisely before another Briton, Tony Jacklin, brought the cup back to England.

TOM WATSON

Born September 4, 1949

Open champion 1975-77-80-82-83 US Open champion 1982
Masters champion 1977-81

No one, not even Vardon, Braid, Taylor, nor Thomson won five Open Championships in the mere nine years it took Tom Watson. It would have been a remarkable rate of success at the easiest of times. Watson achieved it at the hardest, when the fields for the Open were at their most international and at their most formidable.

Like Jack Nicklaus, who had come to power when Arnold Palmer was undisputed king, Watson came to power when Nicklaus had assumed the mantle. Such times are never easy but Watson, by the excellence of his golf and the modesty that accompanied it, followed very much in the footsteps of all the great champions.

It was not easy, particularly in America. He led after

three rounds of the 1974 US Open at Winged Foot but took 79 in the fourth and finished equal fifth. He led after two rounds at Medinah the following year and 'disappeared' again. The Americans had a word for it. Watson was a 'choker'. His critics were not even convinced otherwise when Watson won both the Masters and the Open Championship of 1977 under the severest pressure of all—Nicklaus with all guns firing. At Augusta Watson had led his man by three strokes going into the last round but Nicklaus, playing in the preceding group, came back at him with a 66. It was not good enough. Watson had a 67 and won by two strokes.

Their confrontation at Turnberry in the Open three months later was even more dramatic; both had 68s in the first round and both had 70s in the second. They were paired together on the third day and both holed the course in 65. Playing together again in the final round, Watson had another 65 and Nicklaus a 66.

Coming to the last hole Watson had a one-stroke lead but Nicklaus, from a difficult lie close to some gorse bushes, not only recovered to the green but holed a long putt for a birdie. Watson, from much closer, holed his as well. His 72-hole total of 268 set a championship record.

Watson had been a surprise winner two years earlier at Carnoustie, when he beat Jack Newton, of Australia, in a play-off, but there was an inevitable look about him when he won for a third time at Muirfield in 1980, especially after he had had a third round of 64.

A year later he won the Masters for a second time, again with Nicklaus breathing down his neck but there was an elusiveness about the US Open that was becoming unsettling. At Pebble Beach in 1982 Watson finally laid his apparent bogey, Nicklaus his victim once more.

Watson needed one birdie from the last two holes to overtake Nicklaus, who had already finished, but when he missed the 17th green, it seemed he would do well even to tie. Instead Watson chipped in for a two, had another birdie four at the last and won by two strokes.

Having been leading American money winner for four consecutive years from 1977, there was now no doubt of Watson's standing in the game. He has lacked the consistency of Nicklaus in the major championships—indeed he has still to win the PGA—but his brisk swing and ability to hole telling putts have dominated the Open Championship. He was lucky to win at Royal Troon in 1982, where a young South African, Nick Price, lost a three-stroke lead over the last six holes. But Watson's fifth success a year later at Royal Birkdale saw him hit two of the finest full shots—a drive and two iron—there have ever been to the final green. A four was needed and obtained while the whole golfing world held its breath.

GOLF RECORDS

OVERALL RECORDS

LOW SCORING (MEN)

In winning the Nigerian Open in Lagos in 1981, Peter Tupling, a British professional, returned a world record 72-hole aggregate of 255. However the event was played on browns rather than greens.

In his first big tournament as a professional Sandy Lyle (GB) had opening rounds of 61 and 63 in the 1978 Nigerian Open in Lagos for a 36-hole aggregate of 124.

The lowest score in a national open is held by Gary Player. He had a second round of 59 in the Brazilian Open at Gavea, Buenos Aires, in 1974.

LOW SCORING (WOMEN)

Hollis Stacy had a 72-hole aggregate of 271 in the 1977 Rail Muscular Dystrophy tournament. Kathy Martin had a 36-hole total of 131 in the 1976 Birmingham Classic; as did Silvia Bertolaccini in the 1977 Lady Keystone Open.

Wanda Morgan returned a 60 in an open tournament at Westgate-on-Sea in 1929.

LONGEST DRIVES

The longest drive on a golf course was 515 yards by Michael Austin, of Los Angeles, in the US Seniors Open Championship at Las Vegas, Nevada. The hole measured 450 yards and his ball stopped 65 yards beyond the flag, assisted by a tail wind.

In a long driving competition 'Tommie' Campbell, of Foxrock, Ireland, is credited with a shot of 392 yards at Dun Laoghaire, County Dublin.

Valentin Barios, of Spain, drove a ball 568 yards on an airport runway in Las Palmas.

LONGEST CARRIES

In 1935 W Smithson, professional at Sitwell Park, Rotherham, hit a drive which pitched beyond a ditch 380 yards from the second tee.

George Bell, of Penrith, New South Wales, carried the Nepean River, a distance of 309 yards, in a driving contest.

Francisco, 'Tito', Abreu carried a ditch crossing the 18th fairway at Penina, in the 1972 Algarve Open—a distance of 305 yards.

FEWEST PUTTS

The fewest number of putts in 18 holes is 14 by Colin Collen-Smith at Betchworth Park, Dorking, in 1947. He chipped into the hole four times and single putted the remaining 14 greens.

Richard Stanwood, an American professional, had 15 putts in a round at Riverside, Idaho, in 1976. He chipped into the hole five times.

Fred Taggart, professional at Wilmslow, needed only 20 putts in the first round of the Open Championship at Royal St George's in 1934. He scored a 70.

Boby Wynn had 19 putts in one round of the 1973 Nigerian Open.

The lowest number of putts by a woman is 17 by Joan Joyce in the Lady Michelob tournament in Georgia in 1982.

OLDEST CHAMPIONS

Tom Morris senior was 46 when he won the Open Championship in 1867.

The Hon Michael Scott was 54 when he won the Amateur Championship in 1933.

Mrs Belle Robertson was 45 when she won the British Women's Amateur Championship at Conway in 1981.

YOUNGEST CHAMPIONS

Tom Morris junior was 17 when he won the Open Championship in 1868.

John Beharrell, of England, and Bobby Cole, of South Africa, were both 18 years and one month to the day when they won the Amateur Championship in, respectively, 1956 and 1966.

May Hezlet was 17 years and one week when she won the British Women's Amateur Championship in 1899.

Janet Melville was 20 when she won the British Women's Open Championship in 1978.

Nancy Jupp was 13 when she won the British Girls Championship in 1934, the competition being open to girls of 18 and under.

YOUNGEST INTERNATIONALS

Ronan Rafferty was 16 years and eight months when he represented Great Britain and Ireland in the 1980 World Amateur Team Championship for the Eisenhower trophy. A year later he became Britain's youngest Walker Cup player.

Nick Faldo was Britain's youngest Ryder Cup player, being 20 years and two months for the match at Royal Lytham in 1977.

Jane Connachan, of Scotland, became the youngest Curtis Cup player, being 16 years and three months when she played for Britain in 1980.

The youngest player to represent his country in the World Cup was Marko Vovk, of Yugoslavia, in 1979. He was 15.

HOLES IN ONE

The longest hole at which a hole in one has been recorded was the 480 yard fifth at Hope Country Club, Arkansas, by L Bruce in 1962. The hole is a dog-leg and Bruce drove over the corner.

Robert Mitera holed the longest straight shot for a hole in one, 447 yards at the appropriately named Miracle Hills, Nebraska, in 1965.

In 1964 Norman Manley had consecutive holes in one at par fours, the 330 yard seventh and 290 yard eighth at the Del Valle Country Club, California.

John Hudson, professional at Hendon, had successive holes in one in the Martini tournament at Royal Norwich. The first was an eagle at the 195 yard 11th and the next an albatross at the 311 yard 12th.

In the 1974 Eastern Counties foursomes at Hunstanton, Bob Taylor, of Leicestershire, holed the 188 yard 16th hole on three consecutive days—once in practice and twice in competition.

Mrs AE 'Paddy' Martin had three consecutive holes in one at the 125 yard third hole at Rickmansworth in 1960, each time with the same club and ball, in four days.

HIGHEST SCORE

In a qualifying round for the Shawnee Invitational for women at Shawnee-on-Delaware, Pennsylvania, in 1912, one competitor took 166 strokes at the short 16th hole. Her ball floated down river but, with her husband at the oars, they took to the water and caught up with it one and a half miles downstream. When back on dry land, the only way back to the green was through a wood.

OPEN CHAMPIONSHIP RECORDS

Lowest 72-hole total
268 Tom Watson (68-70-65-65), Turnberry 1977

Lowest 54-hole total
202 Tom Watson (68-70-64), Muirfield 1980

Lowest 36-hole total
132 Henry Cotton (67-65), Sandwich 1934

Lowest first round
65 Neil Coles, St Andrews 1970
65 Bill Longmuir, Royal Lytham 1979

Lowest round
63 Mark Hayes, Turnberry 1977
63 Isao Aoki, Muirfield 1980

Lowest 9 holes
28 Denis Durnian, Royal Birkdale 1983

Most wins
6 Harry Vardon (1896-98-99-1903-11-14)
5 James Braid (1901-05-06-08-10)
5 JH Taylor (1894-95-1900-09-13)
5 Peter Thomson (1954-55-56-58-65)
5 Tom Watson (1975-77-80-82-83)

Most times second
7 Jack Nicklaus (1964-67-68-72-76-77-79)
6 JH Taylor (1896-1904-05-06-07-14)

Youngest winner
17 years 5 months, Young Tom Morris 1868
21 years, Willie Auchterlonie 1893

Oldest winner
46 years 3 months, Old Tom Morris 1867
44 years 3 months, Roberto de Vicenzo 1967

Most victories by amateurs
3 Bobby Jones (1926-27-30)
2 Harold Hilton (1892-97)

Lowest total by an amateur
283 Guy Wolstenholme (74-70-71-68) St Andrews 1960

Biggest winning margin
13 Old Tom Morris, Prestwick 1862

Left-handed champions
Bob Charles, Royal Lytham 1963

Best final round by a champion
65 Tom Watson, Turnberry 1977

Biggest attendance
142,894 Royal Birkdale, 1983

US OPEN RECORDS

Lowest 72-hole total
272 Jack Nicklaus (63-71-70-68), Baltusrol 1980

Lowest 54-hole total
203 George Burns (69-66-68) Merion 1981

Lowest 36-hole total
134 Jack Nicklaus (63-71), Baltusrol 1980

Lowest first round
63 Tom Weiskopf, Baltusrol 1980
63 Jack Nicklaus, Baltusrol 1980

Lowest round
63 Johnny Miller, Oakmont 1973
63 Tom Weiskopf, Baltusrol 1980
63 Jack Nicklaus, Baltusrol 1980

Lowest 9 holes
30 James McHale, St Louis 1947
30 Arnold Palmer, Cherry Hills 1960
30 Ken Venturi, Congressional 1964
30 Bob Charles, Merion 1971
30 Tom Shaw, Merion 1971
30 George Burns, Pebble Beach 1982

Most wins
4 Willie Anderson (1901-03-04-05)
4 Bobby Jones (1923-26-29-30)
4 Ben Hogan (1948-50-51-53)
4 Jack Nicklaus (1962-67-72-80)

Most times second
4 Sam Snead (1937-47-49-53)
4 Bobby Jones (1922-24-25-28)
4 Arnold Palmer (1962-63-66-67)

Youngest winner
19 years 10 months, John McDermott 1911
20 years 4 months, Francis Ouimet 1913
20 years 4 months, Gene Sarazen 1922

Oldest winner
43 years 4 months, Ted Ray 1920
43 years 3 months, Julius Boros 1963

Most victories by amateurs
4 Bobby Jones (1923-26-29-30)

Lowest total by an amateur
282 Jack Nicklaus (71-71-69-71), Cherry Hills 1980

Biggest winning margin
11 Willie Smith, 1899

Left-handed champions
None

Best final round by a champion
63 Johnny Miller, Oakmont 1973

MASTERS RECORDS

Lowest 72-hole total
271 Jack Nicklaus (67-71-64-69), 1965
271 Raymond Floyd (65-66-70-70), 1976

Lowest 54-hole total
201 Raymond Floyd (65-66-70), 1976

Lowest 36-hole total
131 Raymond Floyd (65-66), 1976

Lowest first round
64 Lloyd Mangrum, 1940

Lowest round
64 Lloyd Mangrum, 1940
64 Jack Nicklaus, 1965
64 Maurice Bembridge, 1974
64 Hale Irwin, 1975
64 Gary Player, 1978
64 Miller Barber, 1979

Lowest 9 holes
30 Jimmy Demaret, 1940
30 Gene Littler, 1966
30 Ben Hogan, 1967
30 Miller Barber, 1970
30 Maurice Bembridge, 1974
30 Johnny Miller, 1975
30 Gary Player, 1978

Most wins
5 Jack Nicklaus (1963-65-66-72-75)
4 Arnold Palmer (1958-60-62-64)

Most times second
4 Ben Hogan (1942-46-54-55)
4 Tom Weiskopf (1969-72-74-75)
4 Jack Nicklaus (1964-71-77-81)

Youngest winner
23 years, Severiano Ballesteros 1980
23 years 2 months, Jack Nicklaus 1963

Oldest winner
42 years 5 months, Gary Player 1978
41 years 11 months, Sam Snead 1954

Victories by amateurs
None

Lowest total by an amateur
281 Charlie Coe (72-71-69-69), 1961

Biggest winning margin
9 Jack Nicklaus 1965

Left-handed champions
None

Best final round by a champion
64 Gary Player, 1978

Overseas winners
3 Gary Player (1961-74-78)
2 Severiano Ballesteros (1980-83)

UNITED STATES PGA RECORDS

Match-play 1916-57
Stroke-play from 1958

Lowest 72-hole total
271 Bobby Nichols (64-71-69-67), Columbus 1964

Lowest 54-hole total
200 Raymond Floyd (63-69-68), Tulsa 1982

Lowest 36-hole total
131 Hal Sutton (65-66), Riviera 1983

Lowest first round
63 Raymond Floyd, Tulsa 1982

Lowest round
63 Bruce Crampton, Firestone 1975
63 Raymond Floyd, Tulsa 1982

Lowest 9 holes
30 Art Wall, Llanerch 1958
30 Jerry Barber, Minneapolis 1959
30 Bob Rosburg, Minneapolis 1959
30 Jim Colbert, Firestone 1975

Most wins
5 Walter Hagen (1921-24-25-26-27)
5 Jack Nicklaus (1963-71-73-75-80)
3 Gene Sarazen (1922-23-33)
3 Sam Snead (1942-49-51)

Most times second
4 Jack Nicklaus (1964-65-74-83)
3 Byron Nelson (1939-41-44)
3 Arnold Palmer (1964-68-70)
3 Billy Casper (1958-65-71)

Youngest winner
20 years 5 months, Gene Sarazen 1922
20 years 7 months, Tom Creavy 1931

Oldest winner
48 years 4 months, Julius Boros 1968

Biggest winning margin
7 Jack Nicklaus, Oak Hill 1980 (stroke play)
8 & 7 Paul Runyan beat Sam Snead, Shawnee 1938

Best final round by a champion
65 David Graham, Oakland Hills 1979

Most consecutive matches won (match-play)
22 Walter Hagen

Longest match (match-play)
43 holes Johnny Golden beat Walter Hagen

ALL TIME RECORDS ON THE EUROPEAN TOUR

Lowest 72-hole total
260 Kel Nagle (64-65-66-65), Irish Hospitals 1961

Lowest 54-hole total
194 John Lister, Gallaher Ulster Open 1970
194 Vicente Fernandez, Benson & Hedges 1975

Lowest 36-hole total
126 Tom Haliburton, Spalding tournament 1952
126 Nick Faldo, Lawrence Batley International 1983

Lowest first round
60 Baldovino Dassu, Swiss Open 1971

Lowest 9 hole total
27 Jose-Maria Canizares, Swiss Open 1978

Lowest scoring average
69.03 Nick Faldo, 1983
69.52 Severiano Ballesteros, 1983

Successive birdies
7 Peter Thomson, Dunlop tournament 1958
7 Bernard Hunt, Daks tournament 1958
7 Angel Miguel, Daks tournament 1960
7 Peter Butler, Benson & Hedges 1971
7 Peter Townsend, Viyella PGA 1974
7 Brian Waites, Bob Hope Classic 1980

Successive birdies and eagles
6 birdies and 1 eagle, Jose-Maria Canizares, Swiss Open 1978

Most birdies and eagles in one round
1 eagle, 11 birdies Jimmy Martin, Swallow Penfold 1961

Fewest putts in one round
22 Bill Large, Benson & Hedges qualifying 1972

Most tournament wins
28 Neil Coles; 24 Christy O'Connor;
23 Severiano Ballesteros
(including two world match-play championships)

Consecutive tournament wins
4 Alf Padgham, 1935-36
3 Nick Faldo, 1983

Most tournament wins in a calendar year
5 Nick Faldo, 1983

Most money in a calendar year
£119,416 Nick Faldo, 1983
£99,502 Severiano Ballesteros, 1983
£81,036 Bernhard Langer, 1981
£74,828 Greg Norman, 1980

Most money by a rookie in one year
£38,842 Gordon Brand Jnr, 1982

Biggest winning margin
17 strokes Bernhard Langer, Cacharel Under 25s 1979
15 strokes Peter Thomson, Yorkshire Evening News 1957
12 strokes Guy Wolstenholme, Jeyes tournament 1963

Youngest winner
19 years 4 months, Severiano Ballesteros, Dutch Open 1976
19 years 5 months, Paul Way, Dutch Open 1982

Oldest winner
58 years, Sandy Herd, News of World match-play 1926

ALL TIME RECORDS ON THE UNITED STATES TOUR

Lowest 72-hole total
257 Mike Souchak (60-68 64-65), Texas Open 1955

Lowest 54-hole total
191 Gay Brewer (66 64-61), Pensacola Open 1967

Lowest 36-hole total
126 Tommy Bolt (64-62), Virginia Beach Open 1954

Lowest 9 hole total
27 Mike Souchak, Texas Open 1955
27 Andy North, BC Open 1975

Lowest first round
59 Al Geiberger, Memphis Classic 1977

Lowest scoring average
69.23 Sam Snead, 1950
69.30 Ben Hogan, 1948
69.37 Sam Snead, 1949

Successive rounds under 70
19 Byron Nelson, 1945

Successive birdies
8 Bob Goalby, St Petersburg Open 1961
8 Fuzzy Zoeller, Quad Cities Open 1976

Successive birdies and eagles
6 birdies and 1 eagle, Al Geiberger,
Memphis Classic 1977

Successive birdies to win
5 in the last 5 holes, Jack Nicklaus, Inverrary Classic 1978

Fewest putts in one round
18 Sam Trahan, IVB Philadelphia Classic 1979

Fewest putts for four rounds
94 George Archer, Sea Pines Heritage Classic 1980

Most tournament wins
84 Sam Snead; 69 Jack Nicklaus; 62 Ben Hogan;
61 Arnold Palmer

Consecutive tournament wins
11 Byron Nelson, 1945

Most tournament wins in a calendar year
18 Byron Nelson, 1945

Most money in a calendar year
$530,808 Tom Watson, 1980
$462,636 Tom Watson, 1979
$446,462 Craig Stadler, 1982
$426,668 Hal Sutton, 1983

Most money by a rookie in one year
$237,434 Hal Sutton, 1982
$153,102 Jerry Pate, 1976

Biggest winning margin
16 strokes Bobby Locke,
Chicago Victory Championship 1948
14 strokes Ben Hogan, Portland Invitational 1945
14 strokes Johnny Miller, Phoenix Open 1975

Youngest winner
19 years 10 months, Johnny McDermott, US Open 1911
20 years 4 months, Gene Sarazen, US Open 1922

Oldest winner
52 years 10 months, Sam Snead,
Greater Greensboro Open 1965

MONEY WINNERS

ON THE AMERICAN CIRCUIT

(Up to and including 1983)

1	$4,248,229	Jack Nicklaus
2	$3,103,903	Tom Watson
3	$2,754,185	Lee Trevino
4	$2,387,149	Raymond Floyd
5	$2,372,659	Hale Irwin
6	$2,206,068	Tom Weiskopf
7	$1,930,306	Johnny Miller
8	$1,917,894	Tom Kite
9	$1,885,241	Arnold Palmer
10	$1,691,704	Gary Player (S Africa)
11	$1,684,728	Billy Casper
12	$1,678,444	Lanny Wadkins
13	$1,651,919	Ben Crenshaw
14	$1,626,272	Hubert Green
15	$1,596,827	Miller Barber
16	$1,576,863	Gene Littler
17	$1,492,542	Bruce Lietzke
18	$1,433,845	Jerry Pate
19	$1,429,534	JC Snead
20	$1,378,228	Andy Bean

ON THE EUROPEAN CIRCUIT

1	£502,106	Severiano Ballesteros (Spain)
2	£389,082	Nick Faldo
3	£319,029	Sandy Lyle
4	£307,704	Neil Coles
5	£300,282	Greg Norman (Australia)
6	£277,654	Bernhard Langer (W Germany)
7	£276,227	Brian Barnes
8	£268,075	Sam Torrance
9	£261,813	Manuel Pinero (Spain)
10	£259,948	Bernard Gallacher
11	£231,620	Jose-Maria Canizares (Spain)
12	£225,788	Tony Jacklin
13	£222,374	Mark James
14	£218,756	Graham Marsh (Australia)
15	£206,412	Hugh Baiocchi (S Africa)
16	£197,821	Bob Charles (N Zealand)
17	£196,706	Ken Brown
18	£193,015	Eamonn Darcy
19	£188,707	Brian Waites
20	£178,906	Tommy Horton

These are all time money winners

MAJOR GOLF COURSES

AUGUSTA NATIONAL (Georgia, USA)

Hole		Yards	Par	Hole		Yards	Par
1	White Pine	400	4	10	Camelia	485	4
2	Woodbine	555	5	11	Dogwood	445	4
3	Flowering Peach	360	4	12	Golden Bell	155	3
4	Palm	220	3	13	Azalea	485	5
5	Magnolia	450	4	14	Chinese Fir	420	4
6	Juniper	190	3	15	Fire Thorn	520	5
7	Pampas	365	4	16	Red Bud	190	3
8	Yellow Jasmine	530	5	17	Nandina	400	4
9	Caroline Cherry	440	4	18	Holly	420	4
		3,510	36			3,520	36

Yards 7,030 Par 72

From the bordering Washington Road, with its gas stations, two-hour cleaners, 'donut' counters and profusion of beefburger restaurants, you would have no idea that Augusta National even existed. But turn in the main gate, past the Pinkerton guards, drive up Magnolia Lane towards the low green and white clubhouse and you enter a different world.

Augusta National has one of the smallest and most exclusive memberships in the world. It is even closed for play for several months each year. It is the home of the Masters golf tournament and as such one of the shrines of the game.

No course is more exquisitely prepared, no detail overlooked, no expense spared. It is a living monument to Bobby Jones who, with the expert architectural hand of Alister Mackenzie to guide him, helped to design the course of his dreams, once his playing days were over.

Originally, the gently sloping land, which falls away from the clubhouse, clear of the white tables and chairs on the lawns where the world of golf meets each year, was a nursery. Masters week coincides (or at least is intended to coincide) with the many blooms coming to full flower and the holes are named after them. Under the blue skies of April, it is invariably a picture.

Augusta, with its generous fairways, is not an impossibly difficult course to the average player. Jones never intended it to be so. What it does do, however, is reward excellence. There are safe ways of playing a hole and there are also brave ways. But to be brave you must also be good.

This is particularly evident with the approach shots. From the wrong place on the big, rolling greens, it can be almost impossible to get down in two putts. But from the right place there is very chance of a birdie.

The course begins quite gently, the first test is the

judgement of a short pitch to a 'bowler-hatted' green at the third. Precision is required, too, at the seventh, with its raised green among a nest of bunkers but it is not until the inward half that the drama really unfolds.

Come the final nine holes of the Masters and this is where boys learn to be men, or always stay boys. The 10th, plunging downhill between towering pines, catches the breath with its magnificence, but it is at the 11th that nerve is needed. Appropriately it has a name. Amen corner.

Water eats in to the left of the 11th green; Rae's Creek wanders immediately in front of the short 12th, where players sniff the wind and wonder if it is this club or that, or perhaps even another.

The creek is still there, too, at the mouth of the 13th green, a hole all potential champions are looking to birdie. The conventional way is with a second shot big enough to pitch on the green. At the 15th, too, a big second shot is needed, but this is an even bigger par five, with this time a pond to be carried. This is the hole to watch as the Masters enters its final hour.

But it's not all over even then. More water, almost the full length of the short 16th and then a drive at the 18th through an avenue of trees that can look no wider than the eye of a needle, and at the end of it, a wickedly sloping green that will drain what is left of any physical and emotional reserves.

BALLYBUNION (County Kerry, Eire)

Hole	Yards	Par	Hole	Yards	Par
1	377	4	10	356	4
2	434	4	11	443	4
3	217	3	12	185	3
4	504	5	13	485	5
5	508	5	14	136	3
6	364	4	15	228	3
7	417	4	16	483	5
8	151	3	17	379	4
9	455	4	18	381	4
	3,427	36		3,076	35

Yards 6,503 Par 71

When Tom Watson came back to Britain to defend his Open Championship at Royal St George's, Sandwich, in 1981 he was persuaded by Sandy Tatum, immediate past president of the United States Golf Association, to take a few days off beforehand and just 'play some golf'.

The first course they visited was Ballybunion on the southern shore of the Shannon Estuary. A year later, when Watson came to challenge for the Open again at Royal Troon, winning incidentally for the fourth time, he again arrived early—especially to play Ballybunion.

It is not difficult to understand his enchantment, for Ballybunion has a remoteness and peace about it that must appeal to every genuine golfer's natural instincts. No less a judge than Herbert Warren Wind, America's foremost golf writer, once described it very simply as 'nothing less than the finest seaside course I have ever seen'.

Were it not for the fact that Ballybunion is on the west coast of Ireland, far removed from civilisation, where time has little meaning, where the next landfall is America itself, this is a course which would surely have played host to events of greater significance than just the occasional Irish Championship. It is certainly worthy of better.

Founded in 1896, Ballybunion's tranquillity can often be shattered by some horrendous weather, as the great westerly winds come beating in off the grey Atlantic carrying drenching squalls of rain. On such days a level par round of 71 represents very fine golf indeed.

It is also a much improved course now that the clubhouse has been re-sited. Hitherto it finished with two unimaginative par fives. Now they are the fourth and fifth holes, the 18th being a much more challenging par four through a valley to a green, set in a saddle between two big sandhills.

The start gives little indication of what is to come, a downhill par four, a more testing one uphill between two sentinel dunes, a long par three and then those two par fives before at last one changes direction towards the sea. From then on, or certainly beginning at the seventh, the mind fairly boggles at the beauty of it all.

Towering dunes look down on hole after hole as fairways twist and turn through the valleys, some bordering the very shore of the Atlantic and most of them never very far from it.

Every shot in the book, and more besides, is called for and heaven help the man who is off his game. The seventh, high along the edge of the cliff, may only be marginally outdone by the 11th, which is equally intimidating, while the eighth and 14th are short holes of the highest class demanding absolute accuracy and judgment with the pitching clubs.

Like Cypress Point, Ballybunion has not only successive par fives but as well successive par threes, the 14th and 15th, the latter being as long as its neighbour is short.

There is a wonderfully challenging drive from the 16th tee, the longer and more accurate the shot the better the chance of getting home in two for the birdie that is always useful at this time. The 17th, from another high tee, has the pulse racing and, as one makes tracks for the clubhouse and hospitality as warm as it is Irish, one's only thought is to go out and try again.

Recently Robert Trent Jones, the famous American architect, has been building another course close by that will, he claims, be both bigger and better. It is hard to believe.

CYPRESS POINT (California, USA)

Hole	Yards	Par	Hole	Yards	Par
1	420	4	10	477	5
2	544	5	11	433	4
3	161	3	12	411	4
4	384	4	13	361	4
5	490	5	14	387	4
6	521	5	15	139	3
7	160	3	16	233	3
8	338	4	17	375	4
9	291	4	18	339	4
	3,309	37		3,155	35

Yards 6,464 Par 72

Whenever anyone thinks of Cypress Point, one hole springs to mind, the 16th. A short hole of 233 yards, the tee is set on one promontory of rock and the green on another. Between lies an inlet of the surging Pacific Ocean. It is almost certainly the most spectacular and beautiful hole in golf.

Such is the length of shot to the green, with almost no margin for error, that only the very best players are even able to attempt it. A good many professionals in the Bing Crosby tournament, which Cypress Point shares with Spyglass Hill and the event's headquarters, Pebble Beach, prefer to play the hole as a par four, putting their trust in a pitch from a fairway to the left and much more easily reached.

Yet it would be wrong to say that the 16th is the beginning and the end of Cypress Point. It is a jewel of a course in the most heavenly setting of the Monterey Peninsula, the Pacific on one side and the Del Monte Forest tumbling down the foothills of the Santa Lucia mountains on the other.

Alister Mackenzie, the architect, responded to the finest landscape imaginable and produced a course of great variety—alternately wooded, inland, seaside and cliff-top. When the sky is clear, the sun sparkling on the sea and the sea lions basking on the rocks, it is the sort of place where any golfer would willingly spend the rest of his days.

Only the length of the course and the intense privacy of the club, have prevented it from holding a major championship, though in 1980 Cypress Point did stage the Walker Cup match between the United States and Great Britain and Ireland. Only during the Bing Crosby tournament are the main gates swung open to admit the general public.

An unusual feature of the course is that the fifth and sixth are both par fives and the 15th and 16th both par threes. The eighth and ninth are classic short par fours, twisting high among the dazzling white sandhills and all the time there is the taste of the sea holes still to come.

The 15th, a mere 139 yards, can vary enormously in playing distance, according to the wind. It is played over a small inlet in which the swell of the sea sucks and gurgles and thousands must be the golf balls swallowed at the 16th.

The 17th, a par four, is a marvellous hole as well. The tee is elevated on a promontory of rock behind the 16th green, calling for a bold drive across the sea to a generous fairway, populated by a single pine tree. But it is a most strategically placed tree as the fairway follows the coastline.

Sadly the 18th is an anti-climax, climbing uphill with only the top half of the flag visible for the approach. 'Cypress Point', said Jimmy Demaret once, 'is the best 17-hole golf course in the world'.

DURBAN COUNTRY CLUB
(Natal, South Africa)

Hole	Yards	Par	Hole	Yards	Par
1	390	4	10	550	5
2	182	3	11	456	4
3	506	5	12	147	3
4	172	3	13	337	4
5	459	4	14	514	5
6	349	4	15	166	3
7	383	4	16	375	4
8	498	5	17	392	4
9	424	4	18	276	4
	3,363	36		3,213	36

Yards 6,576 Par 72

Durban Country Club, with the Indian Ocean just the other side of the highway and the tall white buildings of the city standing out against a seemingly permanent blue sky, is as handsome in its setting as it is searching as a test of golf.

By modern standards, it is probably a shade on the short side. But there is infinite variety in the landscape, some holes rising and falling among big dunes covered in thick vegetation, others wending back and forth across flat, gentle fairways.

It is when the wind blows off the sea that the course is at its best, for it puts a strain on shot-making hard enough to examine even the very best players.

George Waterman and Laurie Waters, a former South African Open champion, originally designed the course, opened in 1922. Since then there have been changes, the first of them by Col SV Hotchkin (an architect responsible for one of England's finest inland courses, Woodhall Spa) and more recently by Bob Grimsdell. But despite new tees and a renumbering of some holes, the concept is very much as it was meant to be 60 years ago.

One of the most charming features of the Country Club are the monkeys who survey the golfers with round unblinking eyes, venturing now and then onto the fairways and tees for an unofficial wrestling match, before leaping up some adjacent tree and swinging off into the distance.

There are snakes, too, and it is said that no one spends too long looking for his ball in the bush to the right of the first hole. It is by no means a gentle start while the third hole, from a high tee to a winding fairway below, is one of the finest par fives in the southern hemisphere.

Holes follow on the flat before climbing back among the dunes at the eighth, a strategic rather than long, par five. Then it is back to the flat again before confrontation with the 12th, one of those par threes that depend totally on the tee shot.

On either side of the domed green a steep bank falls away and any shot that does not hold leads to an extremely difficult recovery. It is said that the late Duke of Windsor, a keen and also accomplished golfer, once took 17 there.

Nick Faldo (England).

The 13th, a drive and pitch par four, is a more relaxing hole and it is not until the 17th that the course returns to duneland for a spectacular finish. The drive at the 17th needs to be precisely placed to give a sight of the green while at the 18th there is the chance of driving the green and perhaps holing the putt for an eagle two.

At 276 yards it is an unusually short par four for a finishing hole but with the fairway looking like the swell of some huge wave about to break, and a consequent fall down the deep bank to the right, the drive must be straight and true.

It produced a remarkable finish to the 1928 South African Open, Jock Brews driving the green and sinking a putt of five yards for an eagle two to beat his brother, Sid, by a stroke.

MERION (Philadelphia, USA)

Hole	Yards	Par	Hole	Yards	Par
1	355	4	10	312	4
2	535	5	11	370	4
3	183	3	12	405	4
4	600	5	13	129	3
5	426	4	14	414	4
6	420	4	15	378	4
7	350	4	16	430	4
8	360	4	17	224	3
9	195	3	18	458	4
	3,424	36		3,120	34

Yards 6,544 Par 70

Two of golf's most famous photographs were taken at Merion, which is among the shortest championship courses in the world. The first caught spectators as, in the Fall of 1930, they converged on Bobby Jones after he had taken two putts on the 11th green to beat Eugene Homans by eight and seven to win the American Amateur Championship. His victory completed the Impregnable Quadrilateral, better known as the Grand Slam, since earlier that year he had also won the British Amateur Championship as well as the Open Championships of both America and Britain. Jones never played competitive golf again.

The other famous photograph was of Ben Hogan in 1950 at the completion of his follow-through to a one iron second shot to the 18th green. It earned him a par four and a tie for the United States Open, which he won the following day in a play-off against George Fazio and Lloyd Mangrum.

Not much more than a year earlier Hogan had nearly lost

his life in a car crash. He was still so weak that he had to leave his caddie to pick the ball out of each hole to save him bending unnecessarily. At one point in the afternoon, 36 holes then being played on the final day, he very nearly 'threw in the towel' so much did he doubt his ability to walk let alone play the last few holes. Yet the following day, his fifth round in four days, he holed the course in 69 strokes.

Ten years later, in the world amateur team championship for the Eisenhower trophy, a young amateur by the name of Jack Nicklaus completed four rounds at Merion in a total of 269—18 strokes better than Hogan's score. It was then that the world of golf recognised the great talent that was to burst upon it.

Much golfing history has consequently been written at Merion, a course designed by an immigrant Scot, Hugh Wilson, and frequented more than any other by the United States Golf Association for 'state occasions'. This is in its way remarkable considering the overall lack of length and lack of room in which to manoeuvre big galleries—110 acres and Ardmore Avenue cutting a swathe through its middle, the second to 12th holes being one side of the road and the rest the other.

Two features immediately strike the visitor. The first is that the flagsticks are not topped by flags at all but by oval wicker baskets like small hot-air balloons about to take off to the heavens. The other is the bunkers, once christened the 'white faces of Merion', some 120 in all and many of them dotted with wild clumps of tall, wiry grass.

There are only two par fives, the fourth a massive one of 600 yards. Six of the par fours are of less than 400 yards and one par three, the 13th, only 129 yards, which is only 19 yards longer than the famous short seventh at Pebble Beach.

Merion is therefore a very strategic golf course for it is famous for its fast greens. A well struck shot from the fairway will hold but anything less well struck will not—and certainly almost nothing from the rough.

At the 12th Walter Hagen once struck a putt out of bounds, his ball ending up on the adjacent Ardmore Avenue and the gentle little pitch to the short 13th is very much only half the battle. But it is from then on that Merion bares its considerable teeth.

The last five holes are among the most testing anywhere in the world, strong par fours at the 14th and 15th, a deep quarry to be carried with the second shot at the 16th, a long iron required from the 17th tee and then two thumping blows to the 18th. Such is the carry required from this tee that legend has it that Paul Runyan used first to play a pitch on to a forward tee and play on from there.

In 1981 David Graham played those five holes of the final round of the US Open in two under par. It was a flawless exhibition by the first Australian to win the title.

MUIRFIELD (East Lothian, Scotland)

Hole	Yards	Par	Hole	Yards	Par
1	449	4	10	475	4
2	349	4	11	386	4
3	379	4	12	381	4
4	181	3	13	153	3
5	558	5	14	447	4
6	471	4	15	396	4
7	185	3	16	188	3
8	444	4	17	542	5
9	495	5	18	447	4
	3,511	36		3,415	35

Yards 6,926 Par 71

Muirfield is the home of the Honourable Company of Edinburgh Golfers who, in 1872, joined with the Royal and Ancient and another Scottish club, Prestwick, in helping to run the Open Championship each year. Hitherto organisation had been in the sole hands of Prestwick. The three clubs took it in turns to stage the championship before Sandwich, Hoylake and then Deal were introduced. Not until 1919 did the Royal and Ancient assume complete control of the the Open.

The club is recognised as being the oldest in the world, its records going back to 1744 and indeed containing the 13 original rules of the game. In those days the Honourable Company played at Leith, a five-hole course, before moving to Musselburgh, which staged a number of Open Championships, and then in 1891 to Muirfield on a lovely stretch of coast overlooking the Firth of Forth.

It was here in 1892 that the Open Championship was first extended from 36 holes to its present 72 and since then the club has played constant host to all the principal British events, for men and women alike, and also international occasions like the Ryder, Walker and Curtis Cups.

Many believe, and with some justification, that Muirfield is the finest course in the British Isles. It certainly impressed Jack Nicklaus. It was here that he played in the 1959 Walker Cup and here again that he won the Open Championship for the first time in 1966, thereby completing his first set of the four 'majors'. When subsequently he designed a course of his own in Ohio, he called it Muirfield Village.

From the spectators' point of view it is almost the perfect watching course. It runs clockwise for nine holes and then anti-clockwise, within the outward half, for the second nine.

The furthest point is no more than two holes from the clubhouse and with only one exception (the third, fourth and fifth) do more than two holes follow the same direction.

The direction of the wind has therefore to be taken into constant account. More often than not it comes blowing off the Forth, where ships head either west towards Edinburgh or east to the North Sea. At Archfield Wood, close by the eighth green and ninth tee, the trees are bent double in seemingly constant battle with the weather.

Yet Muirfield is not quite a links. It is more compact than sprawling but there is a wonderful spring to the turf as the land falls gently towards the shore, Fife clearly visible across the water. Some of the greens are quite small and all the bunkers as deep as they are beautifully contoured, gathering any shot that elsewhere might escape.

It is a driver's course. When Henry Cotton won the Open here in 1948 he missed four fairways in 72 holes. When Nicklaus triumphed in 1966, he put his trust very much in a one iron from the tee. The rough is much more lush and therefore more punishing than at many seaside courses.

There are only three par fives and the shortest of them, the ninth, the best. A deep wedge of rough leaves only a narrow landing area and the second shot has to be played half towards a low, grey-brick wall, out-of-bounds beyond.

The 13th is a wonderful, tightly bunkered, short hole with a green set in the dunes and the 17th made famous by Lee Trevino when, in the 1972 Open, he chipped in to retrieve a title he had mentally conceded to Tony Jacklin.

Henry Cotton (England).

PEBBLE BEACH (California, USA)

Hole	Yards	Par	Hole	Yards	Par
1	379	4	10	424	4
2	306	5	11	382	4
3	395	4	12	204	3
4	327	4	13	393	4
5	170	3	14	565	5
6	516	5	15	395	4
7	110	3	16	403	4
8	433	4	17	209	3
9	467	4	18	548	5
	3,302	36		3,523	36

Yards 6,825 Par 72

Just around the headland from Cypress Point, lies Pebble Beach, a majestic course sweeping along the shore of the lovely Carmel Bay and the site, in 1972 and 1982, of two American Open Championships. It has also played host to two United States Amateur Championships, the first in 1929 and the other in 1961.

That there have not been more Open Championships has been due to a reluctance by the United States Golf Association to use courses not within easy reach of a major city. Yet each time they have ventured to this particular shore of the Pacific, a particular corner of history seemed to be turned.

In 1929 it was the defeat of Bobby Jones in the first round of the US Amateur, thereby ending six successive appearances in the final, five of which he had won. If America was stunned then, so it was in 1961 when Jack Nicklaus won the title for the second time in three years, his awesome power and talent seeing him win by nine and eight in the semi-final round and by eight and six in the final. A year later he was American Open Champion.

Then, in 1972, Nicklaus became the first American to have won both the Amateur and the Open on the same course. Ten years later, at the age of 42, it seemed he was about to triumph again. But Tom Watson, a thorn in Nicklaus's side so often in the late afternoon of his career, chipped in for a birdie two at the 17th to draw ahead in the most unlikely of circumstances. At the 18th Watson made another birdie and won by two strokes.

Few American courses so approach the character of a British links, though by no means all of it. The first taste of the sea does not come until the fourth, a tight drive-and-pitch hole but the spectacular stuff begins at the long sixth where the cliffs tumble down to rocks battered by constant surf.

The seventh is a dream of a short hole, a mere 110 yards and hardly even a nudge with the wedge on a still sunlit day. But when the wind is up and the spray coming in clouds across the green, sometimes even a three iron has not been enough.

The eighth, too, catches the breath; a drive to a rising fairway that comes to an abrupt halt some 240 yards from the tee and then a second shot clean across a chasm in the cliffs to a green seemingly perched on a ledge the other side.

Next come two magnificent par fours along the cliff edge with the fairways tipping dangerously towards the beach below. It is little wonder that Robert Louis Stevenson once described this particular stretch of coast as 'the greatest meeting place of land and water in the world'.

Some form of respite comes as the next six holes make their way back inland through the edge of the Del Monte Forest towards the Lodge where the millionaires take their vacations. The climax comes at the 17th and 18th.

The 17th is a brute of a par three with the green seemingly somewhere out to sea, though of course it is not. Then comes the final sting to the tail, a glorious finishing hole, 548 yards stretching along the shore inviting players to bite off just that little bit more than they can chew with their drives.

There is no club as such at Pebble Beach and tarred tracks to take the golf carts have scarred its natural beauty. But Jack Neville, the architect, produced as good a test of golf in 1920, when the course was opened, as it is today, more than 60 years later.

PINE VALLEY (Philadelphia, USA)

Hole	Yards	Par	Hole	Yards	Par
1	427	4	10	145	3
2	367	4	11	399	4
3	185	3	12	382	4
4	461	4	13	446	4
5	226	3	14	185	3
6	391	4	15	603	5
7	585	5	16	436	4
8	327	4	17	344	4
9	432	4	18	424	4
	3,401	35		3,364	35

Yards 6,765 Par 70

Nobody playing Pine Valley for the first time—and probably

most other times as well—is allowed to set foot on the course without a caddie. Nor is it advisable, he quickly learns not to drive until his caddie has instructed the general line of the shot and then advanced a suitable distance so that hopefully he can see exactly where the ball lands.

There then follows an elaborate pre-arrangement of signals, rather like semaphore, by which caddie will indicate to golfer whether it is safe for him to proceed. There are basically three signals: the first that the ball is in play and on mown grass; the second that it is not on mown grass and therefore only *may* be in play; and the third that it very definitely is not in play, re-load and try again.

The members at Pine Valley have long had a standing bet that no one will break 80 first time out. They have lost from time to time—notably when Arnold Palmer, then American Amateur Champion and a young man in need of the money, had a 68—but for the most part they are betting on a certainty.

Pine Valley was best described as being 'a 185-acre bunker', broken up by islands of tees, fairways and greens. Between these islands lie sandy wastes, so vast that no attempt is ever made to rake them or keep them tidy. Once off the fairways, there is a gnawing feeling that it may never be possible to get back on them.

It is almost certainly the hardest inland golf course in the world and surrounded by the most unprepossessing country-side imaginable. It tcok seven years to build but such was the vision of George Crump, a hotelier from Philadelphia, who died shortly before the course of his dreams was completed, that he created the ultimate in a golfing oasis.

A lot of the course's difficulty is psychological, born of legendary tales in which otherwise strong men were brought in off the course weeping with frustration. As much as anything it demands a cool head.

The most famous story concerns a local amateur, Woody Platt. He started with a birdie three, very much of a bonus as the hole dog-legs sharply right, and then at the second, where the approach has to be hit over a sea of sand and scrub to an elevated green surrounded by wasteland, he sank a seven iron for an eagle two.

It is a case of the green or nothing, at all of Pine Valley's four short holes and at the third Platt holed in one. At the fourth, a long and twisting par four with one fairway at the receiving end of the drive and another fairway at the receiving end of the second shot, he got home in two and then holed the putt for a birdie.

After four holes Platt was therefore six under par. By chance the green is close by the elegantly furnished clubhouse—like Cypress Point you might almost be in an English country hotel—and Platt decided to refresh himself, if only to steady his nerves. He stayed there for the rest of the day.

There are only two par fives at Pine Valley—the seventh

and 15th—but so genuine are they that nobody has ever reached either green in two shots. They are both in the region of 600 yards in length, one hopping and skipping across stepping stones of fairway and the other crossing a lake before climbing remorselessly uphill through a shrinking avenue of trees and bush.

Because of its hopelessness as a watching course, Pine Valley's only claim to fame was the 1936 Walker Cup match. But there was wide rejoicing when the club was awarded it again for 1985.

PORTMARNOCK (Dublin, Ireland)

Hole	Yards	Par	Hole	Yards	Par
1	388	4	10	380	4
2	368	4	11	445	4
3	388	4	12	144	3
4	460	4	13	565	5
5	407	4	14	385	4
6	586	5	15	192	3
7	180	3	16	527	5
8	370	4	17	466	4
9	444	4	18	408	4
	3,591	36		3,512	36

Yards 7,103 Par 72

Ireland is blessed with many fine courses, from Royal County Down and Portrush in the north to Ballybunion and Rosses Point in the west and Killarney somewhere in the middle. Portmarnock, not far from the city of Dublin, is certainly the equal of any of them and, in the eyes of some, better.

It is a true links, lying on a peninsula with the Irish Sea on one side and tidal mud flats on the other, over which in the dim and distant past the golfers used to make their way; either by boat at high tide or by horse-drawn cart when the waters were on the ebb.

Now a narrow road leads to the low, white clubhouse but it is a good mile from what one might call the main highway between Sutton and Malahide and the remoteness and peace of Portmarnock is therefore faithfully preserved.

Such are the horrific bottlenecks on high days and holidays like the Irish Open, which has been played here on a number of occasions, that there has been talk of supplementing this single track with a bridge to ease congestion. But so far the conservationists have prevailed.

In some ways Portmarnock, a big course in that it measures in excess of 7,000 yards with a standard scratch score of 75 (three more than the par), resembles Muirfield in the east of Scotland. It has much the same compactness, the ninth hole for instance coming back to clubhouse which is unusual for a links. Mostly, as with the Old Course at St Andrews, it is simply a case of 'out and back'.

Another similarity is the repeated change in the direction of the holes. Occasionally, as with the third and fourth, it is only a subtle change but enough to make the golfer think as he sniffs the wind, mostly from the west and blowing therefore out to sea towards a pile of remote rock known as Ireland's Eye.

Portmarnock opens gently enough with a par four along the edge of the mudflats. The second and third should demand little more than pitches to the green though the drive at the latter does have to be held left to avoid straying into some marshy ground at the rounded point of the peninsula.

Shoulders must begin to be opened at the fourth, where the green is partly hidden behind the bulge of a dune and the sixth can play very long, sometimes even three wooden

Arnold Palmer (United States).

club shots to a raised, sloping and tightly bunkered green.

Not the least endearing aspect of Portmarnock is the quality of its three short holes. The seventh, from a high tee to a well defended green, is no exception while the 12th is a little beauty, the green up in the sandhills, all curves and slopes and surrounded by deep pot-bunkers.

From the 13th tee one gets a marvellous panoramic view along a stretch of golden beach and south towards Howth Hill which, on its other side, overlooks Dublin Bay. From then on the going gets tough, long par fives in similar direction at the 13th and 16th and, in between, a classic par four to a slippery green and an examining par three tight along the shore with all manner of trouble to anyone who misses the target.

The 17th, invariably into the prevailing wind, is almost a par four-and-a-half and the 18th, now shorter than once, set in a pleasing amphitheatre with a steep slope fronting the green and an awkward little swale behind. Portmarnock is the complete test.

ROYAL ST GEORGE'S (Kent, England)

Hole	Yards	Par	Hole	Yards	Par
1	445	4	10	375	4
2	376	4	11	216	3
3	214	3	12	362	4
4	466	4	13	443	4
5	434	4	14	508	5
6	156	3	15	467	4
7	529	5	16	165	3
8	415	4	17	425	4
9	387	4	18	458	4
	3,442	35		3,419	35

Yards 6,841 Par 70

Royal St George's, just outside the ancient port of Sandwich, was the first English course to stage the Open Championship. That was back in the dim and distant past of 1894 when JH Taylor won with a score of 326, not once breaking 80 in any of his four rounds.

From then until 1949, when Bobby Locke won the first of his four titles, these noble links on the shores of the Strait of Dover, played a prominent and regular part in the development of championship golf. But for the next 32 years, so far as the Open was concerned anyway, Royal St George's was removed from the small and exclusive group of venues.

This was due almost entirely to the lack of access for the increasingly large crowds that descended on the Open through the sixties and seventies. The quaint little streets of Sandwich would have created impossible bottlenecks of traffic and it was not until a by-pass was built that the Royal and Ancient turned again to Royal St George's for the Open of 1981. It was an immediate success and due to be staged there again in 1985.

There was nevertheless a certain amount of scepticism from the players. They tended to regard the course as too old-fashioned in that the many humps and hollows that are such a feature of the fairways presented an unfair proportion of difficult stances and therefore shots.

Frank Pennink, the architect, consequently made a number of improvements to the land first spotted in the 1880s by Dr Laidlaw Purves as suitable for a golf course. He built a new short third hole beside the original, which had demanded a totally blind shot to the green, made the eighth into an attractive par four where before it had been a par three very similar to the sixth, or Maiden as it is known, and reduced the 11th from a par four to a par three.

For all these changes, Royal St George's has lost none of its charm. The sky there seems bigger than anywhere else and when the sun is shining on the waters of Pegwell Bay, the larks singing and the breeze whispering through the gently waving grass on the big sand dunes, there is a rare feeling of this being golf as it used to be.

Many ghosts still walk the links, from Taylor to Walter Travis, an Australian-born American who, in 1904, became the first overseas player to win the Amateur Championship; from Walter Hagen, who in 1922 won his first Open here, to Bobby Jones, captain of the first American Walker Cup team to win on English, as opposed to British, soil.

It was at Sandwich, too, that Henry Cotton, in 1934, set a record Open score of 65 that was not beaten for more than 40 years en route to the first of his three championships and here, too, that Jack Nicklaus had his first win in Britain, the St George's Challenge Cup when he was a member of the visiting American Walker Cup team.

Throughout the holes constantly change direction but it is the last six that dig deepest into a golfer's reserves. The 13th is a strong two-shotter up towards the clubhouse at neighbouring Princes, the 14th is known as Suez because of the canal that crosses the fairway and the 15th a marvellous long par four to a narrow green falling in waves to the right.

Tony Jacklin's hole in one at the 16th in the 1967 Dunlop Masters was the first to be recorded by television and the 18th as good a finishing hole as anywhere in Britain, a bunker at the entrance of the green on the right and a teasing little swale to the left.

ST ANDREWS (Fife, Scotland)

Hole		Yards	Par	Hole		Yards	Par
1	Burn	370	4	10	Bobby Jones	342	4
2	Dyke	411	4	11	High	172	3
3	Cartgate	398	4	12	Heathery	316	4
4	Ginger Beer	463	4	13	Hole O'Cross	425	4
5	Hole O'Cross	564	5	14	Long	567	5
6	Heathery	416	4	15	Cartgate	413	4
7	High	372	4	16	Corner of the Dyke	382	4
8	Short	178	3	17	Road	461	4
9	End	356	4	18	Tom Morris	354	4
		3,528	36			3,432	36

Yards 6,960 Par 72

The Old Course at St Andrews was to golf a gift of nature. Quite simply, it happened; created by the wind, the sea and even the sheep as they sought shelter from the elements by burrowing into little pockets of sand, thus building bunkers that still exist today. No course owes less to man, has changed less in the two, three or even four hundred years golf has been played there (the Royal and Ancient club was formed in 1754 but there is written evidence of golf being permitted in 1552), nor survived so well the passage of time.

It is the home of golf, the seat of government that lies within the greystone clubhouse of the Royal and Ancient, which overlooks the first and 18th holes and, to the right, the great sweep of St Andrews Bay. Every golfer the world over dreams one day of making his pilgrimage and every golfer has his chance. No introductions are needed. The course is public, requiring only a modest green fee.

It was here that the terms 'out' for the first nine holes and 'home' for the second nine were first used. The Old Course follows a narrow ribbon of linksland out to the shores of the Eden Estuary, loops round at the turn and then comes home, retracing footsteps made in the opposite direction. So narrow is it still that only the first, ninth, 17th and 18th holes have their own greens. All the rest are double greens, a hole out sharing one with another coming home.

Consequently the greens are vast and it is little indication of how a man has played if he reports that he 'hit every green in regulation'. It could easily have meant his three and four-putting quite regularly across slopes so wickedly undulating from the wrong places that it would have been a miracle for him to have got down in only two putts.

Not one hole can even claim to have a fairway of its own.

These, too, are shared but such is the proliferation of bunkers that a round of golf is not unlike threading one's way through an ever changing minefield. However well one may know the course, bunkers appear that one could swear had never been there before, appearing as if by magic overnight.

Consequently no round of golf is safely over until the last putt is holed. However serene the progress, however sweetly the ball is flying out of the middle of the clubface, potential disaster lurks at every step.

An example was in 1970 when Tony Jacklin began his defence of the Open Championship by going out in 29. But he drove into a bush at the 14th just as a violent storm broke, had to leave his ball there for the night, ultimately took seven and was never quite the same again.

Similar disasters have occurred on every one of the Old Course's 18 holes, beginning at the first. No opening tee shot can be less inhibiting across the broad expanse of the first and 18th fairways, though strong men still shake from head to foot, aware of unseen eyes, if not ghosts from the past as well, watching silently from within the clubhouse.

The second shot over the Swilcan burn is the first test for it is always one club, perhaps two or even three more than you think it is. It is a relief to get out to the seventh, the beginning of the famous loop. For six holes no hole is longer than 372 yards and two of them are par threes. This is the moment to make a score. Equally a card can be ruined as when Gene Sarazen took six at the 11th in defence of his Open Championship in 1933, three of them in a bunker.

Perhaps the most testing hole coming home is the 17th where many a man has been on the green in two, bunkered in three and on the road beyond in four. Even the broad acres of the 18th have claimed its victims, most of them out of the Valley of Sin at the front of the big green under the pitiless stare of the ever present St Andreans leaning on the railings.

Bobby Jones (United States).

SOTOGRANDE (Costa del Sol, Spain)

Hole	Yards	Par	Hole	Yards	Par
1	394	4	10	453	4
2	527	5	11	373	4
3	339	4	12	582	5
4	235	3	13	214	3
5	361	4	14	503	5
6	517	5	15	426	4
7	422	4	16	388	4
8	199	3	17	174	3
9	363	4	18	440	4
	3,357	36		3,553	36

Yards 6,910 Par 72

In the past 20 years golf has developed all over the world, not least in Spain where the warm climate, particularly during the European winter months, attracts an increasing number of visitors from all over the continent, the British Isles and even beyond.

All along the Mediterranean coast new courses have sprung out of the ground to cope with the army of golfers that descend out of the skies, borne by a variety of airlines. But it is doubtful whether any of them is regarded with quite the same respect as Sotogrande.

Some 20 miles from Gibraltar, whose massive rock climbs out of the sea to west, Sotogrande was the first architectural venture in Europe by Robert Trent Jones. There are two courses, the Old and the New, but it is the former that springs first to most people's minds. Many regard it as Trent Jones's finest work.

With the sea on one side and a low range of mountains on the other, the setting is a very appealing one, as the course winds between the twisted cork trees, rising gently uphill for nine holes and then turning slowly back to an elegant clubhouse with its group of neighbouring villas, all whiter than white in the brilliant sunshine.

The greens, though large, are not as severely contoured as on some Trent Jones courses but constant watering is needed to keep them alive during the long hot summers, so too on the fairways on which the ball sits up and begs for a clean hit with the brassie.

No one needs to stand on the first tee 'cold'. A fine practice ground lies alongside. The shoulders have to be opened at the second but there is always the chance of a birdie for the long hitters as there is, too, at the third and fifth, two short par fours where the key lies in the placement of the drive and then a controlled pitch.

The sixth, another par five, is almost a double dog-leg. The seventh, Sotogrande's most photographed hole, has a fairway tumbling down into a valley, requiring an inviting if perilous second shot to an angled green bordering a lake. It is a most satisfying hole from which to depart with a four under the belt.

Having reached the high point of the course, there is a challenging drive from the 10th tee over trees for the big hitters and the 12th, 13th and 14th border a lake which, in its time, has claimed its fair share of victims. The 14th, a par five of just over 500 yards, can be reached in two shots but it is necessary to carry a dangerous amount of water to do so.

Another lake, man made though it hardly appears so, guards both the 16th and 17th greens, the penultimate hole demanding from the tee a medium iron that must be hit clean across the water if the pin is to be attacked. Golf at Sotogrande, as indeed is true of all the watered Spanish courses, has more in common with the game in America than it does in Britain.

It is played 'through the air' as opposed to 'along the ground'—one of the reasons why as a country it has produced of recent years so many fine players, from the Miguel brothers to Ramon Sota and his celebrated nephew, Severiano Ballesteros.

SUNNINGDALE (Surrey, England)

Hole	Yards	Par	Hole	Yards	Par
1	494	5	10	478	5
2	484	5	11	325	4
3	296	4	12	451	4
4	161	3	13	185	3
5	410	4	14	509	5
6	415	4	15	226	3
7	402	4	16	423	4
8	182	3	17	421	4
9	267	4	18	414	4
	3,111	36		3,432	36

Yards 6,543 Par 36

The British Isles is blessed not only with noble links, where the Open Championship is by tradition always held, but also by some lovely heathland courses far removed from the sea. The Surrey and Berkshire area west of London is one such fertile area and the loveliest of all, the Old Course at Sunningdale.

Such is the modest yardage by modern standards that there is a tendency not to regard it as championship golf. However it is within 36 inches of the length of Merion, which staged the US Open as recently as 1981, and by any standards is a splendid example of heathland golf with its heather, pine and silver birch and a fine spring to the turf.

It was here in 1926 in a qualifying round for the Open Championship that Bobby Jones played what has been described as the perfect round of golf, a 66 that was nothing but fours and threes, 33 shots and 33 putts. It was his shot-making through the green that drew the superlatives, for most of his approach play was done with the brassie and two iron. Yet he hit them with an accuracy and precision normally reserved for the much shorter clubs.

More than half a century later the course is still a good test. Certainly holes have been lengthened but the design by Willie Park has stood the test of time like the magnificent oak tree, now the club's emblem, which stands ever more proud as it throws its shadow across the 18th green.

Technically there are four par fives, the first, second, 10th and 14th but only the latter should extend the long hitters. However this is a course that demands subtlety and control of the ball rather than power, for the heather which borders the fairways can indeed be penal.

The opening to the course is not a demanding one and there should be chances of birdies at each of the first three holes. The real enchantment begins at the fifth.

There are few finer views in England than that down a ribbon of fairway between the heather, a small pond just short of the green and then the sixth fairway disappearing through the trees into the haze of a summer morning. It is a photographer's haven.

The seventh is picturesque as well, with its domed fairway and a green set in the side of a hill. A great surge of strength envelopes the golfer as he surveys the 10th fairway far below him; already the aroma of coffee and hot sausages teasing his senses from the Half-way House behind the distant green.

For a short par four, the 11th is an absolute classic, with its slightly raised green causing mental anguish over the safer shot to play—the chip and run or the delicate little pitch.

The 12th green tumbles out of a heathery hill, demanding quite a long second shot while the 13th, from its lofty tee, is cunningly defended by a grassy swale on three sides. The 15th, another short hole, is both much longer and more demanding from a sheltered tee to an exposed green. They say that anyone who finishes 3,4,4,4 at Sunningdale is seldom beaten.

WOMEN'S GOLF

Lewine Mair

There are those who will tell you that women golfers have become a much harder species since the advent of women's professional tours, both in America and in Britain. That may well be so, but the fact remains that even the earliest exponents of the game were not always the gentle and ladylike souls they seemed. By the late 1800s, the extent to which women's golf was catching on in all corners of the British Isles prompted one worried gentleman to declaim: 'The fever of golf, when it takes hold of a woman, is relentless. She manages to forget her worst domestic tragedies, her best friends and even her manners'

When the American women professionals came along—their association was founded in 1950—the emphasis was very much on theory. Indeed, these globe-trotting professionals are nowadays so far into technique that the conversations at their championships are often of little else.

Nancy Lopez is something of an exception in this respect in that she has never liked to delay her departure after a round. Nancy did for the LPGA tour what Olga Korbut did for the world of gymnastics when, in 1978, she won five LPGA tournaments in a row. Asked to explain Nancy's appeal, the LPGA's tournament director, Betsy Rawls, caught it perfectly when she said, 'It's not just that Nancy is pretty. It's that she is pretty in everything she does. She has a certain attraction that I haven't seen before. It's a combination of being a good player, being a winner and possessing a charm that is warm, personable and persuasive.'

Nancy Lopez (United States).

The pioneers of the women's tour included such as Patty Berg, Marilynn Smith and Louise Suggs. The legendary Babe Zaharias, who won two gold medals at the 1932 Olympics before going on to win one American Amateur Championship and three American Opens, did much to make the new circuit newsworthy and, at the same time, set new standards in terms of practice. In her autobiography, the Babe recalled hitting ball after ball until her hands were sore and bleeding: 'I'd have tape all over my hands and blood all over the tape.'

At the present time, Mickey Wright and Kathy Whitworth stand out for having won more than 80 tournaments apiece, while one player to have enjoyed a long and illustrious spell at the top of both the amateur and professional game is Jo Anne Carner. The winner of five American Amateur titles and two American Opens in a career spanning three decades, she in 1982, at the age of 43, won five LPGA events and demolished the all-time LPGA money-winning mark with comfortably more than 300,000 dollars.

Jo Anne also feature four times in the Curtis Cup, the annual Anglo-American match founded by Harriet and Margaret Curtis in 1932 and won by the Great Britain and Ireland side only in 1952 and 1956.

If the Curtis Cup is without doubt the best-known match in the world of amateur golf, the Vagliano Trophy is not far behind. A biennial fixture between the golfers of Great Britain and Ireland and those of Europe, the contest was never better than in the late sixties and early seventies when Catherine Lacoste was featuring at the head of the Continental side.

An incorrigible and immensely likable French girl, Miss Lacoste, or Catherine de Prado as she now is, has in her time won each of the world's top titles—namely, the American Open, the American Amateur and the British Women's Championship.

Of the three, the American Open is the most important in that it is the highlight of the strongest women's professional circuit on the golfing globe. There is a thriving professional tour in Japan which has produced Chako Higuchi of the swaying swing and Ayako Okamoto, but the standard in those parts is by no means as high as in the States. The top Japanese girls tend to graduate to the American tour as, of course, do the leading players from other lands, with Australia's Jan Stephenson and South Africa's Sally Little perhaps the most eye-catching imports on the LPGA circuit.

Results in the Curtis Cup explain why it is that the American women's Amateur Championship gets the No 2 billing in a ranking list of premier events on the distaff side. Yet, in spite of its strength, there are few winners of that title who would not consider their amateur careers to be the better for a British Match-Play championship.

In 1976, the Ladies Golf Union of Great Britain turned their British Amateur Stroke-Play Championship into a British Open Stroke-Play Championship. Golfers on both sides of the Atlantic hoped that this would build up into an event on a par with the men's British Open. As yet, this has not happened. But no-one doubts that it will, for it was one of Mark McCormack's men who said, recently, 'there is no tournament in the world —either men's or women's—with such potential.'

THE RULES OF GOLF

When in the final round of the 1977 Open Championship at Turnberry Jack Nicklaus holed a long putt for a birdie across the 18th green, it left his opponent, Tom Watson, with a putt of around a yard for a three as well and victory by a stroke.

After two days of riveting cut and thrust between them (Watson playing the last two rounds in 65 and 65 and Nicklaus in 65 and 66) this was the ultimate climax and the vast crowd was in a ferment of excitement. To still the cheers, Nicklaus held up his hands for quiet so that Watson could concentrate totally on the putt that would, and did, beat him.

Herein lay perhaps the finest example of golfing etiquette, or good manners. It is the first essential of the game for without it golf would be lost. Consideration for others and total honesty are as important as the ball itself.

Few games are easier at which to cheat. More times than not the player is his only witness. A foul shot can go totally undetected, such as one by Arnold Palmer in the 1961 Open at Royal Birkdale. His ball moved as he was addressing it in a bunker. The world as a whole was oblivious. Palmer alone knew. He reported it, turned a 72 into a 73 and still went on to win. He could not otherwise have lived with himself.

Yet for all golf's simplicity, the ball being struck from an appointed place until it is holed out in a hole four and quarter inches in diameter, usually between 100 and 600 yards away, the rules are both lengthy and complex. They have been amended and re-written many times by both the Royal and Ancient and the United States Golf Association and in 1984 they were reorganised into what was claimed to be a simpler form.

A total grasp of the many complexities of the rules is still beyond most people and even those well-versed occasionally have to seek guidance from the Rules of Golf Committee, who then issue decisions. These have become the size of a large book.

The rules book itself runs to a length of 80 pages and fits easily into the pocket or golf bag and all golfers should have one, just as they should, too, have a grasp of the major points.

Etiquette comes first, covering as it does consideration for others. For instance no one should move, talk or stand close to, or directly behind, the ball when another player is addressing the ball with the intention of making a stroke.

The game should also be played without delay, though not before those in front are out of range. If it is clear that a ball will not be easily found, players behind should at once be invited to play through.

When a hole has been completed, players should leave the green immediately and it is helpful if they have left their clubs at the side of the green nearest to the next tee.

Singles, a game between two players, should, in the absence of a special rule of the day such as a competition, have priority and be allowed to pass any three or fourball

The following is a synopsis of the Rules of Golf, which are the copyright of the Royal and Ancient Golf Club of St. Andrews and the United States Golf Association.

match. A single player has no standing.

Care of the course is important. Players should smooth out the sand after playing out of bunkers, footprints as well; they should replace divots, repair pitch marks on the greens and also obvious damage caused by spikes.

In addition to the rules of golf, club committees may also introduce what are known as local rules; these would cover abnormal playing conditions such as the existence of mud on the course, the accumulation of fallen leaves, stones in bunkers, staked trees and abnormal damage to the course.

THE GAME

Rule 1 Playing the ball from the teeing ground into the hole by a stroke or successive strokes is the basis of the game. No player may influence the position of the ball except in accordance with the rules. Players may not agree to waive any rules.

Rule 2 In *match-play* a hole is won by the side which completes a hole in fewer strokes or, in a handicap competition, in the lower net score. A hole is halved when the two scores are the same. The match is over when one side is more holes up than there are left to play.

Rule 3 In *stroke play* the winner is the competitor who completes the stipulated round or rounds in the lowest score; in a handicap competition, the player who has the lowest net score.

When in doubt over procedure, a competitor may also play a second ball. He should hole out with both balls and report the facts to the committee, who will decide which score should count.

If a player fails to hole out before playing from the next tee or, in the case of the last hole of a round, before he has left the putting green, he is automatically disqualified.

CLUBS AND BALL

Rule 4 A player may start a stipulated round with no more than 14 clubs. He may, if he starts with fewer, add as many as will bring the total to that number, though not if it will unduly delay play.

A club damaged in the normal course of play may be replaced but neither addition nor replacement may be done by borrowing from another player on the course. Partners may share clubs provided that between them they have no more than 14.

Rule 5 The size of the ball shall not be less than 1.62 inches in diameter. In an increasing number of competitions the larger 1.68 inch ball has become mandatory.

If a ball becomes unfit for play, either because it is out of shape or cut, it may immediately be replaced—but only if the player gives his opponent or marker the opportunity first to examine the ball.

PLAYER'S RESPONSIBILITIES

Rule 6 It is advisable for a player to put an identification mark on his ball. When marking a card in stroke-play, he should check his partner's card after each hole. Only the gross score for each hole need be written down. The addition is the responsibility of the committee.

No alteration to the card may be made after it has been handed in. It must be signed by both player and marker. If the player signed for a score at any hole lower than actually taken, he is disqualified. If he signs for a score higher than that taken at any hole, the score returned shall stand.

Players may, of their own accord, stop play only when they consider themselves endangered by lightning, or because of sudden illness. Leaving the course does not constitute discontinuance of play.

Rule 7 Practice on the course is allowed only before a *match-play* competition. In *stroke-play* practice putting and chipping is allowed on or around the green of the hole just played (not from a hazard) and also on and around the tee of the next hole.

Rule 8 A player may seek advice only from his partner (in foursomes or fourball) or from either of their caddies. But in team competition advice may be received from such as the captain or coach, with prior approval of the committee.

The line of play may be indicated from anyone for a shot through the green. On the green the line of a putt may be indicated only by partner or caddie but the green must not be touched.

ORDER OF PLAY

Rule 10 In *match-play* the honour on the first tee should be decided by draw, or by lot. The side which wins a hole takes the honour on the next tee. Through the green, the ball furthest from the green must be played first, otherwise an opponent may ask it to be replayed, without penalty.

In *stroke-play*, the rules are the same as in match-play

except that a shot played out of turn will not be recalled. A putt may be played out of turn.

TEEING GROUND

Rule 11 The ball must not be played in front of the two tee-markers, nor more than two clubs length behind. If the ball is knocked off a tee peg at the address, there is no penalty.

PLAYING THE BALL

Rule 12 In a search for the ball, only as much rough as is necessary may be moved to identify the ball. If it is covered by loose sand in a hazard, only as much sand as necessary may be brushed away to enable part of the ball to be seen.

Rule 13 The ball shall be played as it lies, except as otherwise provided in the rules or local rules. In a hazard a player's club may not touch the ground or a loose impediment other than in playing the stroke. There is no penalty for playing a wrong ball in a hazard.

Rule 14 A stroke is a forward movement of the club with the intention of striking the ball, whether the ball moves or not. If the player strikes the ball more than once in playing a stroke, he shall add a penalty stroke, making two strokes in all.

Rule 15 In *match play*, if a player plays the wrong ball, except in a hazard, he shall lose the hole. If both players strike the wrong ball, the first to do so will lose the hole.

In *stroke-play*, If a player hits the wrong ball, other than in a hazard, he will add two penalty strokes. For more than one stroke with the wrong ball he is not additionally penalised. However, if he fails to realise his mistake before driving off at the next hole, he is disqualified.

PUTTING GREEN

Rule 16 Loose impediments may be brushed away from the line of a putt. Pitch marks and old hole plugs may be repaired. A ball on the green may be marked, lifted and cleaned. It is not permissible to make a stroke while standing astride the line of a putt or with either foot on an extension of a line of the putt behind the ball.

FLAGSTICK

Rule 17 The player has the option of having the flagstick attended, removed or held up. When putting from the green, if his ball strikes the flagstick, he is penalised by two strokes in stroke-play and loses the hole in match-play.

BALL MOVED, DEFLECTED OR STOPPED

Rule 18 A ball is deemed to have moved if it comes to rest in another place. If it has already come to rest and is moved by an outside agency, it shall be replaced without penalty.

If the ball is moved by the player, his caddie, partnér or equipment (other than permitted by the rules) he is penalised a stroke and must replace the ball. There is no penalty for moving the ball when searching for it in a hazard.

If the ball moves while a player is addressing it, he is penalised a stroke; similarly if it moves while removing a loose impediment, though in this case the ball must be replaced.

In *match-play* if a ball is moved by his opponent, caddie or equipment, other than during a search, the opponent shall incur a penalty stroke. In *stroke-play* the ball shall simply be replaced, without penalty.

If a ball at rest is moved by another ball, it shall be replaced.

Rule 19 If a ball in flight is deflected or stopped by an outside agency, it shall be played as it lies. If in *match-play* it is deflected or stopped by the player, his equipment or caddie, he shall lose the hole. In *stroke-play*, if the ball is similarly deflected or stopped, he incurs a penalty of two strokes.

In *match-play*, if an opponent deliberately deflects or stops the player's ball, the opponent loses the hole. But if it strikes an opponent accidentally, the shot may either be played as the ball lies or replayed without penalty to either side.

A fellow competitor, caddie or equipment accidentally struck by a moving ball in *stroke-play* is considered an outside agency.

A ball in motion which hits a ball at rest is played as it lies without penalty. In *stroke-play*, if both balls lie on the green the player who putted incurs a penalty of two strokes.

RELIEF SITUATIONS AND PROCEDURE

Rule 20 If, under the rules, a ball may be lifted and then replaced, its position must first be marked. If the ball is to be dropped, the player shall stand erect, hold the ball at arm's length and drop it, though not nearer the hole.

It must be re-dropped if it rolls into a hazard, out of a hazard, onto a putting green or out of bounds, back into the position from which relief was taken or more than two club lengths from where it first struck the ground. If this happens again the ball should then be placed.

Rule 21 A ball may be cleaned after suspension of play; for identification; on the green; for relief from an artificial obstruction; for relief from abnormal ground conditions; for relief from a water hazard and after relief from an unplayable lie.

Rule 22 A ball may be lifted if a player considers it will assist another player or he can have another ball lifted if he considers it will interfere with his next stroke.

Rule 23 Other than in a hazard, loose impediments may be removed.

Rule 24 If a ball lies close to a moveable obstruction, the obstruction may be moved. If it lies in or on the moveable obstruction, the ball may be dropped without penalty after the obstruction has been moved.

Rule 25 A ball lying in casual water—a temporary accumulation of water—or on ground under repair, may be lifted and dropped without penalty. In casual water within a hazard, a player may either drop the ball still in the hazard without penalty or outside the hazard at a penalty of one stroke.

A ball lying in casual water on the green may be lifted without penalty, as it can when casual water interferes with the line of a putt, provided the ball is already on the green.

A ball embedded in its own pitch mark on any closely mown area of the course may be lifted and dropped without penalty. It is compulsory to take relief if the ball lies on the wrong putting green, including a practice green.

Rule 26 If a ball is lost in a water hazard, another ball, at a penalty of one stroke, shall be dropped behind the hazard, keeping the point of entry by the original ball between the player and the hole. Or the shot can be replayed, under penalty.

If a ball is lost in a lateral water hazard another ball is dropped at a penalty of one stroke within two club lengths of the point where the original ball crossed the margin of the hazard, not nearer the hole. Or the shot can be replayed, under penalty.

Rule 27 If a ball is lost outside a water hazard or is out of bounds, another ball shall be played, under a one-stroke penalty, from the spot where the original ball was played.

If a ball may be lost or out of bounds, a provisional ball shall be played from the original place immediately and may continue to be played until the player reaches the place where the original ball is likely to be. Provided the original ball is lost or out of bounds the provisional ball then becomes the ball in play. If the original ball is found, the provisional ball is taken out of play, any strokes with it not counting.

Rule 28 The player may declare his ball unplayable anywhere except in a water hazard. He is the sole judge of the unplayable lie. He then has three options: to play his next shot from the original place; to drop the ball within two club lengths of the place where the ball lay but not nearer the hole; or drop behind the spot where the ball lay, keeping that spot between himself and the hole, going back as far as he likes.

A ball is lost if it is not found within five minutes, though a player has no obligation to look for it and may put another ball immediately into play.

Peter Thomson (Australia).

HANDICAPS

Handicaps are based on a player's average score above the Standard Scratch Score of his home club. The SSS is basically decided by a course's overall length.

yards	SSS	yards	SSS
7,001-7,200	74	5,451-5,700	67
6,801-7,000	73	5,201-5,450	66
6,601-6,800	72	5,001-5,200	65
6,401-6,600	71	4,801-5,000	64
6,201-6,400	70	4,601-4,800	63
5,951-6,200	69	4,401-4,600	62
5,701-5,950	68	4,201-4,400	61

There are four categories of handicap:
Category 1 up to 5
Category 2 6 to 12
Category 3 13 to 20
Category 4 21 to 28

Handicaps are increased by 0.1 of a stroke for every medal round —not stroke or strokes—in which the player's net score (his actual score less handicap) fails to equal the SSS. This also applies to a no return.

Handicaps are decreased according to category:

category	**playing handicap**	**above SSS add only**	**below SSS subtract for each stroke under**
1	Up to 5	0.1	0.1
2	6 to 12	0.1	0.2
3	13 to 20	0.1	0.3
4	21 to 28	0.1	0.4

On an upward graph, as soon as a player's handicap reaches 0.5 (say 12.5), his playing handicap is increased to 13 but his actual handicap will continue to be adjusted from 12.5.

On a downward graph, as soon as the same player's handicap reaches 0.4 (11.4 for example), his playing handicap is reduced to 11 but his actual handicap will continue to be adjusted from 11.4.

GLOSSARY OF TERMS

Ace Hole in one.
Address The position a golfer takes before beginning his swing.
Air shot An unsuccessful attempt to make contact with the ball.
Albatross A score of three below par on one hole, for example a two at a par five.
Amateur An amateur golfer is one who plays the game solely as a non-remunerative and non profit-making sport. Prizes or prize vouchers may not exceed a value of £150 in Great Britain and Ireland; and not more than $350 US elsewhere, unless that country's governing body decides on a lesser amount.
Approach A shot to the green.
Apron The immediate surround to a green, the grass being cut shorter than on the fairway but not as short as on the green.
Arc The plane, or path, through which the club is swung.
As it lies Once the ball has been driven from the tee, it must be played 'as it lies' unless it is lost, unplayable or relief is allowed through the Rules of Golf or a club's local rules.
Auction sweepstake When club members bet on either themselves or fellow members in a certain competition, the highest bidder being obliged to offer a half share to the player(s) he has backed.
Away The player whose turn it is to hit the ball next, being furthest from the green. It need not always apply when putting.
Backdoor A putt which falls into the hole from the far side, otherwise known as 'the tradesman's entrance'.
Backswing The movement of the club away from the ball.
Baffy A now extinct hickory or wooden-shafted club roughly the equivalent of the modern four-wood.
Bandit A golfer regarded by others to play regularly below his current handicap.
Baseball grip Hands close together, though neither overlapping nor inter-locking.
Bent A fine texture of grass used mostly in the sowing of fairways and greens.
Bermuda A coarse grass, common on fairways and greens in hot climates.
Better-ball See **fourball.**
Birdie A score of one under par on one hole.
Bisque A handicap stroke taken at a hole of a player's choice, provided play of the next hole has not started.
Bogey In Britain the number of strokes with which a good player was expected to complete a hole. Tends now to refer to one over par.
Borrow Striking a putt which allows for the slope of a green.
Bunker A crater in the ground filled with sand. A player may not ground his club before playing a shot, even at the address.
Bye A friendly match between two, three or four players when the original game is over. For instance if one side wins seven and six, the bye is played over the last six holes.
Caddie A man, or woman, who carries a player's clubs. A

professional caddie is expected to offer advice but any golfing rules broken will penalise the player.
Carry The distance a ball travels through the air.
Casual water Water lying on the course after heavy rain or flooding. Also applies to snow and ice.
Chip A short, low stroke normally played just off the green.
Cleek A hickory-shafted equivalent of the modern two iron.
Cock A bending of the wrists usually during completion of the backswing; uncocking takes place when hitting the ball.
Concede A putt or shot so close to the hole that the opponent does not ask it to be holed. He may also concede a hole when he considers himself certain to lose it.
Course rating The evaluation of a course's difficulty compared to other courses. This provides uniformity to the handicapping system.
Croquet putting Swinging the putter between the legs, as in croquet. Ruled illegal in 1967.
Cup The hole in which the flag is placed.
Cuppy A very small depression in which the ball lies.
Cut A shot which moves from left to right, usually intentional.
Dead A shot or approach putt very close to the hole.
Divot Piece of turf uprooted in playing a shot.
Dormie A player is dormie when he is as many holes up as there are holes left to play. It does not apply if the conditions of the competition stipulate extra holes.
Double eagle American expression for an albatross, three under par at a particular hole.
Draw Intentional shot when the ball moves from right to left.
Drive The shot from the tee, normally played with the driver.
Duck hook Unintentional shot which bends sharply right to left.
Duff Unintentional shot when the player hits the ground behind the ball.
Eagle A score of two under par at one hole.
Eclectic A competition played over a number of rounds when the player counts only the lowest score at each hole. Otherwise known as a Ringer score.
Equity A decision not covered by the rules.
Face The surface of the club designed for striking the ball.
Fade An intentional shot which moves from left to right.
Fairway Closely mown grass between the tee and green.
Feathery The original ball made of stuffed feathers and encased in leather.
Feel Artistry and touch in the playing of a successful stroke.
Fescue A finely bladed grass common on good greens.
Five-day member One who can play only between Monday and Friday.
Flight The trajectory of the ball.
Fluff Like the duff, hitting the ground behind the ball.
Follow-through The path of the club head after striking the ball.
Fore A warning shout to other players in danger of being hit by a ball in flight. It may also urge those ahead that they are

holding up play.
Forecaddie A 'ball spotter' at blind holes.
Forward press A slight forward movement, usually instigated by a left to right movement of the right knee, immediately before beginning the backswing.
Fourball Two golfers playing as a team, the lower score at each hole counting.
Foursome Two players partner one another. Player A drives at the odd holes, player B at the even holes. Shots are then played alternately.
Freeze A seeming inability to take the club head back, most common over a short putt when under pressure.
Gimmie A putt short enough to be conceded, even though in stroke-play it would still have to be holed.
Goose neck A bend in the shaft of a putter, close to its head, so that the shaft is slightly in front of the head.
Greensome A mixture of foursomes and better-ball play. Two players again partner one another and both drive. They then have the choice of which ball to play, A playing B's ball or *vice versa* at each hole. Shots are then played alternately.
Gross The number of strokes taken to complete a hole or round.
Ground under repair An area of ground defined by the club or tournament committee from which a player may remove his ball and drop it clear without penalty.
Half A hole is halved when, in match-play, the scores are the same.
Half shot A shot played with less than a full swing.
Handicapping A method of making all players equal. If the standard scratch score of a course is 72 a scratch player should complete his round in 72, an eight handicap player should complete his round in 80 and a 22 handicap player complete his in 94. He then subtracts his handicap from his gross score. This is called his net score.
Hazard A bunker, pond, river or ditch.
Head up A tendency among golfers to see where the ball has gone an instant before they hit it. Otherwise known as 'looking up'.
Heavy Hitting the ground a fraction before the ball, thereby losing distance.
Heel The part of the face of the club nearest the shaft.
Hickory A wooden-shafted club.
Home of golf St Andrews.
Honour The player whose turn it is to drive first at any one hole.
Hooding club Turning the face of the club inwards so as to reduce the loft in an effort to keep the ball low.
Hook A shot which keeps bending left.
Hosel The socket into which the club shaft is fitted.
Hustler A player who likes to gamble when he knows the odds are in his favour.
In The inward half, or second nine holes.
In to out A stroke in which the clubhead, at impact, is travelling

to the right of the target.
Interlocking grip When the little finger of the right hand is entwined with the first finger of the left, or *vice versa* for a left-hander.
Jigger A largely obsolete club with the loft roughly of a four iron, used for recoveries from bad lies. Still occasionally used for chipping.
Knuckles The number of knuckles visible on a player's left hand when he addresses the ball.
Lateral A lateral water hazard runs parallel with the line of play, it not being practical to drop a ball behind this hazard keeping the spot at which it last crossed the margin between the player and the hole.
Lie Where the ball comes to rest.
Line The intended direction in which the ball will be struck.
Links A seaside course.
Lip The edge of the hole.
Local rules Rules appertaining to a particular course. The removal of stones from bunkers, is an example.
Loft Variation in the angle of the clubhead to give the ball greater or lesser height in flight.
Loop A short sequence of holes which loop back to much the same place.
Lost ball A ball is lost if it has not been found within five minutes of the search beginning. It may also be declared lost without looking for it.
Marker Normally a fellow competitor who marks the card of the golfer with whom he is playing. When the numbers are odd, a scorer can be appointed.
Mashie An old fashioned mid iron, roughly the equivalent of a five iron.
Match-play When holes are won by the fewer strokes taken, the winner being more holes up than there are holes left to play.
Medallist An American expression for the winner of a stroke or match-play event.
Medal play When the scores are recorded at each hole and added up at the completion of a round.
Metal wood A club of wooden-headed design made of metal.
Method Style of play.
Mixed foursomes The same as foursomes except that a man and a woman are partners.
Municipal course A course owned by a local authority and one on which anyone can play on payment of a green fee. Called a public course in the USA.
Nap More common in hot climates where coarse grass on the greens tends to make putts deviate.
Nassau A form of betting when a sidestake is settled beforehand. But when one side becomes two up, the other can 'press' and a second and concurrent game begins at that point. Four and five games can therefore take place within the original game.

Net A player's score after he has subtracted his handicap allowance.
Niblick An old fashioned wedge.
Nineteenth The first extra hole in match-play, or the bar in the clubhouse.
Observer An assistant to a referee whose main task is to keep ahead of a match and to see that no one interferes with the ball when or before it comes to rest.
Overlapping grip The most widely-used grip, as popularised by Harry Vardon. The little finger of the right hand overlaps the first finger of the left.
Out The outward half, or first nine holes.
Out of bounds Normally beyond the perimeter of the course. The shot must then be played again from the same place, counting the original stroke plus a penalty stroke.
Pacing A recent development whereby a player paces out distances to the green from certain points.
Par Par is governed by a hole's yardage. A hole of up to 250 yards is a par three, between 251 and 475 yards a par four, and 476 yards and more a par five.
Penalty stroke A stroke added to a player's score under the Rules of Golf.
Pick out Picking the ball out of an unplayable lie.
Pin high A shot level with the flagstick, though not necesarily on the green.
Pitch A short high approach shot to the green.
Pitch and run A low shot that rolls rather than pitches and stops.
Playing out of turn Playing a stroke when it was the turn of the opponent or, in foursomes, a partner's turn.
Playing the like A British term for playing the stroke which will equal the number of strokes played by the opposing side.
Playing the odd A British term for playing the stroke which will be one more than those played by the opposing side.
Play-off When two or more players tie, they play off over a given distance, either over 18 holes, or, more commonly these days, by sudden death—the first player to win a hole.
Plugged ball A ball which imbeds itself in its own pitchmark.
Plus handicap A plus handicap player is one who is expected to score lower than the standard scratch score. He adds rather than subtracts his handicap to his gross score.
Pot bunker A small, deep bunker.
Practice swing A swing with no intention of striking the ball.
Preferred lies Mostly applied in winter when courses are wet. A player may then move his ball, normally not more than six inches from its original position without penalty.
Pull A shot which goes left of the target.
Push A straight shot but one which goes to the right of the target.
Quick Description of a player whose swing gives the impression of being hurried.
Rap A short, sharp putting stroke.

Rhythm A recurring smoothness of swing, without apparent hurry or effort.
Rolling A tendency to turn the shoulders on too much of a horizontal plane, thereby throwing the swing out of line.
Rough Otherwise known as jungle, rhubarb, cabbage and tiger country, it is the part of the course left to nature—neither tee, nor fairway, nor green nor hazard.
Round 18 holes.
Rub of the green A chance deflection of the ball, kind or unkind.
Run The course of the ball after it has stopped bouncing. A fast-running course indicates hard ground, normally associated with summer conditions.
Run-up A low chip shot.
Rutting iron A now extinct club once used for difficult lies in ruts or cracks in the ground.
Sand iron A broad-soled, very lofted club used for getting the ball out of bunkers. Often used as well from heavy rough.
Sand trap Modern variation of a bunker, more a shallow saucer of sand, often very large, common to new courses.
Sclaff Old Scottish term for hitting the ground behind the ball.
Scratch A player who consistently matches the standard scratch score of more than one course; his handicap is then scratch.
Shag bag American expression for a bag in which a player puts his practice balls.
Shank Otherwise known as a socket, the ball is struck by the part of the club nearest the hosel and flies off at right angles. A dreaded 'disease' among golfers, it normally is associated with short pitches and chips.
Short A player who hits the ball a less than average distance.
Short game Chipping and putting around the green; the little shots to the flag.
Shot Stroke
Singles A game between two players.
Slice Usually an unintentional swerve on the ball which keeps on bending to the right.
Socket See **shank.**
Sole The part of the club which rests on the ground when a player addresses the ball.
Square Short for all square, when a match is level. Also refers to a method of play in which the club head is held at right angles to the line of play throughout the stroke, neither opening on the backswing nor closing on the follow-through.
Stableford Form of competition in which points are awarded for the number of strokes taken at each hole. One over par gets one point, level par two points, one under three points, two under four points and three under five points. Most common in handicap competitions.
Standard scratch score The number of strokes in which a scratch player is expected to complete the course. Overall length of the whole course is the governing factor.
Staying down The ability to hit 'through the ball' without lifting

the head or 'quitting' on the shot.
Stroke index A chart on the scorecard which shows on which holes the handicap player will receive his handicap strokes; essential in either match-play or stableford competitions.
Sudden death When two or more players finish level at the end of the competition and then play extra holes until one wins.
Stymie When one ball lay, and could be left, directly between another ball and the hole on the green. This was called 'laying a stymie' and was once part of match-play. It was declared illegal in 1951.
Sway A tendency to move the head laterally when swinging the club.
Swing weight The weight of the club head which a golfer feels when he swings the club. The weight is adjustable.
Take away First movement of the club away from the ball.
Target golf Infers a wet course with soft greens on which the ball will stop quickly; like a dart into a board.
Tee A plastic or wooden peg on which the ball is placed on the teeing ground. The teeing ground is also known as 'the tee'.
Temporary green An emergency green mostly used in winter to save the proper green from being unnecessarily damaged.
Texas wedge A putter; called a Texas wedge only when it is used from off the green.
Thin A shot hit on the leading edge of the sole of the club.
Threeball Three players, each with his own ball, competing against each other.
Threesome Two players in partnership, hitting alternate shots with the same ball as in foursomes, against one player hitting his own ball.
Through the green Everywhere on the course except on the teeing ground and the green of the hole being played.
Tight course One with narrow fairways.
Toe The part of the clubface furthest from the shaft.
Top Hitting the top of the ball so that it runs along the ground.
Trap American description of a bunker.
Trouble Mostly refers to a shot into the rough.
Twitch An involuntary jerky putting stroke, most common close to the hole.
Up A player is up when he has won more holes than his opponent.
Upright A swing which is nearer to a vertical than a horizontal plane.
Vardon grip Popularised by Harry Vardon, the little finger of the right hand overlaps the first finger of the left; *vice versa* for left handers.
Waiting for it The ability not to hurry the swing.
Water hazard A lake, pond, river, ditch or sea.
Wedge A very lofted club used for shots over trees, bushes and bunkers and the shorter approach shots.
Wry neck A golf club on which the head is set slightly behind the shaft.

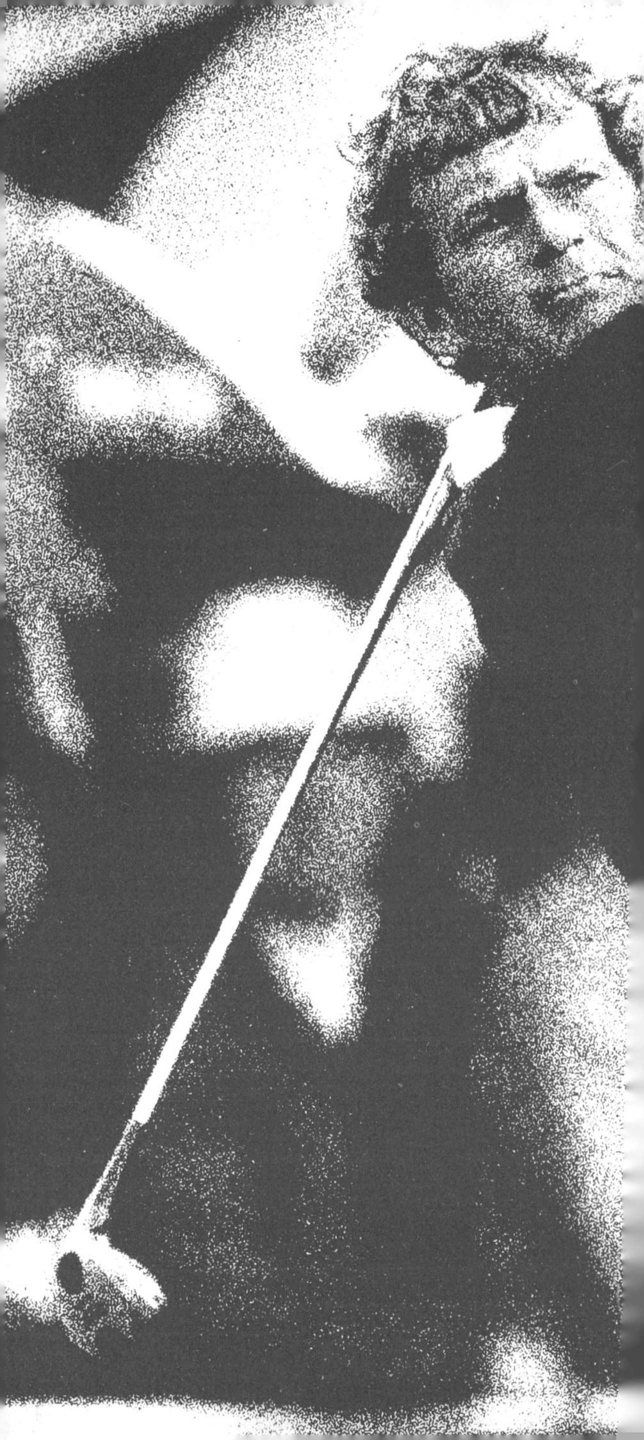